THE FAMILY IN SEARCH OF A FUTURE

SOCIOLOGY SERIES

John F. Cuber, *Editor*

Alfred C. Clarke, *Associate Editor*

THE FAMILY
IN SEARCH OF A FUTURE

Alternate Models for Moderns

Edited by

HERBERT A. OTTO, Ph.D.
The National Center for the Exploration of Human Potential

APPLETON-CENTURY-CROFTS
EDUCATIONAL DIVISION
MEREDITH CORPORATION

New York

ACKNOWLEDGMENTS
    Special acknowledgment to McCall Corporation for permission to reprint the article: "Marriage in Two Steps," Margaret Mead, Ph.D. *Redbook Magazine,* July, 1966 (reprinted on pp. 75-84).

    Special acknowledgment to Lancet Publications, Inc., for permission to reprint the article: "Polygyny after 60," Victor Kassel, M.D. *Geriatrics,* vol. 21, April, 1966, pp. 214-218 (reprinted on pp. 137-144).

    Special acknowledgment to Dick Fairfield for permission to reprint the article: "The Cold Mountain Farm," Joyce Gardener, *Modern Utopian,* August, 1967 (reprinted on pp. 189-200).

Preface

Four of the papers in this collection were originally presented at the American Psychological Association's 1967 Annual Meeting in Washington, D.C., as a part of a symposium called Alternate Models For The American Family Structure. The four symposium members, Alpenfels, Greenwald, Jourard, and Satir, made some changes and additions in their presentations. The other papers in the collection (with two exceptions) are original contributions written for this volume by scientists in the forefront of their fields. The idea of the symposium was suggested by my colleague, Dr. Leonard Pearson, who unfortunately could not participate in the book.

As editor, I am particularly pleased that the range of styles and diverse viewpoints expressed offer the reader an excellent balanced introduction to current attempts to think through and present alternatives to monogamy and the prevailing family structure.

Miss Elissa Schroeder, in her role as editorial assistant, made an outstanding contribution and offered many ideas, as did Roberta Otto. I am also indebted to many of my colleagues and friends for their support and encouragement throughout the creation of this volume.

H. A. O.

Notes on Contributors

DR. ETHEL J. ALPENFELS is Professor of Anthropology in New York University's School of Education. She is the author of *Sense and Nonsense about Race* (New York, Friendship Press, 1965) and of "The Anthropology of the Human Hand." Her other writings have included articles in *The American Journal of Nursing*, *The Educational Record*, *Scholastic Magazine*, *Parent Teachers Magazine* and *Instructor Magazine*.

DR. JOHN F. CUBER is Professor of Sociology at Ohio State University, Columbus, Ohio. He has published over thirty-five articles in such professional journals as *American Sociological Review*, *American Journal of Sociology*, *Marriage and Family Living*, and *Social Forces*. His published books include *Marriage Counseling Practice* (New York, Appleton-Century-Crofts, 1948); *Problems of American Society*, 4th ed. (New York, Holt, Rinehart & Winston, 1964); and *The Significant Americans: A Study of Sexual Behavior Among the Affluent* (New York, Appleton-Century-Crofts, 1965).

DR. JOSEPH J. DOWNING is a psychiatrist now serving as Program Chief of the San Mateo County Health Services and as a member of the planning committee of the San Mateo Youth Conservation Program. He has published over forty articles in various magazines and journals devoted to the improvement of community mental health and has held positions in varied professional associations, including the American Public Health Association, the American Psychiatric Association, the American Orthopsychiatric Association and the California Conference of Local Mental Health Officers.

DR. ALBERT ELLIS is Executive Director of the Institute for Rational Living and the Institute for Advanced Study in Rational Psychotherapy. A leader in the field of sexual liberalism, he has published more than twenty-five books and monographs, and over 250 papers for such journals and anthologies as the *American Psychologist*, *American Journal of Psychiatry*, *Journal of Consulting Psychology*, *American Sociological*

Review, and *The American Journal of Psychotherapy.* He has served as associate editor of *The International Journal of Sexology, Journal of Marriage and the Family, Journal of Sex Research, Voices: The Art and Science of Psychotherapy,* and *Existential Psychiatry.*

DR. HAROLD GREENWALD of New York City has a private practice in individual and group psychotherapy, serves on the faculty of the Metropolitan Institute for Psychoanalysis and is consultant to the Pride of Judea Treatment Center. He is president of the National Psychological Association for Psychoanalysis and author of *The Call Girl: A Social and Psychoanalytic Study* (New York, Ballantine, 1958); *Great Cases in Psychoanalysis* (New York, Ballantine, 1959); *The Active Psychotherapies* (New York, Atherton Press, 1966); and co-author of *Emotional Maturity* (New York, Harper Brothers, 1960).

DR. EDWARD C. HOBBS is Professor of Theology and Hermeneutics in the Graduate Theological Union and the Church Divinity School of the Pacific; and also Lecturer in Medicine (Philosophy of Medicine) in the University of California School of Medicine (San Francisco). He has acted as Visiting Professor at the Pacific School of Religion and as Lecturer in Philosophy in the University of California (Davis). He is past president of the Society of Biblical Literature, and past chairman of the New Testament Colloquium. His books include: *Book of the Judges of Israel* (Chicago, Ill., University of Chicago Press, 1950); *A Stubborn Faith* (Dallas, Texas, S.M.U. Press, 1956); and *Wesley Order of Common Prayer* (Nashville, Tenn., Abingdon Press, 1957). He has contributed chapters to *Christian Faith and the Contemporary Arts* (Nashville, Tenn., Abingdon Press, 1962); to *The New Testament Today* (Berlin, Knoll Verlag, 1964); and others. He has published numerous articles and reviews in such publications as *Texte und Untersuchungen zur Geschichte der altchristlichen Literatur, Kristano Bulteno, Perkins Journal, Motive, Journal of Religion, Anglican Theological Review, Journal of Bible and Religion* and *Religious Education.*

DR. SIDNEY M. JOURARD is Professor of Psychology at the University of Florida. Past president of the American Association for Humanistic Psychology, Dr. Jourard has conducted seminars and workshops at Esalen Institute. He has published articles in the *Journal of Abnormal Social Psychology, Journal of Consulting Psychology, Journal of Humanistic Psychology, Journal of Existential Psychiatry,* and *Review of Existen-*

tial Psychology and Psychiatry. His books include *Personal Adjustment: An Approach Through the Study of Healthy Personality* (New York, Macmillan, 1958), *The Transparent Self* (Princeton, Van Nostrand, 1964), and *Disclosing Man To Himself* (Princeton, Van Nostrand, 1968).

DR. VICTOR KASSEL has conducted an intensive private practice of geriatrics since 1951. He is a Fellow of the Gerontological Society, and a Fellow of the American Geriatrics Society. Formerly Chief of the Geriatric Unit of the Salt Lake Veterans Administration Hospital, Dr. Kassel is a Board Member of the Utah Council on Aging, and served as a delegate to the White House Conference on Aging in 1961. He has been affiliated with the University of Utah Medical School, as instructor in its Departments of Medicine and Psychiatry, and with the Wyoming State Hospital as consulting geriatrician. His articles have appeared in such publications as *Geriatrics, Journal of American Geriatrics Society*, and the *Rocky Mountain Medical Journal.*

DR. CARL LEVETT is a psychologist practicing in White Plains, New York, and in Ridgefield, Connecticut. Formerly Director of White Plains' Family Relations Center, Dr. Levett has served as a free-lance group leader in projects seeking to develop human potentialities, and as a consultant for Planned Parenthood.

DR. MARGARET MEAD is Curator of Ethnology for the American Museum of Natural History, and Adjunct Professor of Anthropology at Columbia University. Her publications include articles in *Science, The American Anthropologist, The American Scholar*, the *Journal of Orthopsychiatry*, and the *Harvard Business Review.* She has written the books: *Coming of Age in Samoa* (1928); *Growing Up in New Guinea* (1935); *Sex and Temperament in Three Primitive Societies* (1935); . . . *and Keep Your Powder Dry* (1942); and *New Lives for Old* (1956), all published by William Morrow & Co., New York; and *Continuities in Cultural Evolution* (New Haven, Conn., Yale University Press, 1964).

DR. GERHARD NEUBECK is affiliated with the University of Minnesota as Professor of Family Studies, assistant director of the Family Study Center, and director of the school's Marriage Counseling Training Program. He has contributed articles to such publications as *Journal of Marriage and the Family*, the *International Journal of Comparative Sociology, Personnel and Guidance Journal, Marriage and Family Living, The Journal of College Student Personnel Work* and *ACTA Sociologica.*

He has written chapters for the books *Marital Counseling: Psychology, Ideology, Science* (Springfield, Ill., Charles C. Thomas, 1967); and *Ways of Growth* (New York, Grossman, 1968).

DR. HERBERT A. OTTO is Chairman of the National Center for the Exploration of Human Potential, La Jolla, California. He has published over forty articles in such journals as *Journal of Marriage and the Family, Mental Hygiene, The Psychiatric Quarterly, Social Casework* and the *International Journal of Social Psychology*. He is editor of *Explorations in Human Potential* (Springfield, Ill., Charles C. Thomas, 1966) and *Human Potentialities: The Challenge and The Promise* (St. Louis, Warren H. Green, 1968); and co-editor with John Mann of *Ways of Growth* (New York, Grossman, 1968). His own books include *Guide To Developing Your Potential* (New York, Charles Scribner's Sons, 1968); *Group Methods Designed to Actualize Human Potential* (Chicago, Ill., Achievement Motivation Systems, 1967); and *More Joy in your Marriage* (New York, Hawthorn Books, 1969).

DR. GEORGE S. ROSENBERG is Associate Professor in the Department of Sociology at Case Western Reserve University, Cleveland, Ohio, and director of the school's Social Gerontology Program. He has published in *History and Theory*, and his latest book, *Poverty, Aging and Social Isolation*, will be published by Jossey-Bass, Inc. of San Francisco. Another volume, *Indicators of History*, will be published shortly thereafter.

VIRGINIA SATIR is Director of Training for the Family Project at the Mental Health Research Institute of Palo Alto, California, and consultant to family research projects and training programs throughout the United States. She has introduced approaches derived from her own experience as a family therapist and from research at the Mental Research Institute to workshops and clinics in Europe and Israel. She has served as director of the Esalen Institute Residential Program and has published widely in professional magazines and journals. Her most recent book is *Conjoint Family Therapy* (Palo Alto, Ca., Science & Behaviour Books Inc., 1965).

DR. FREDERICK H. STOLLER is Associate Professor in the School of Public Administration at the University of Southern California, and Senior Research Associate of the school's Youth Studies Center, as well as Training Consultant for UCLA's Clinical Psychology Training

Program. He has published papers in *American Psychologist, Psychology Today*, the *International Journal of Group Psychotherapy, Federal Probation, Journal of Research and Development in Education, American Behavioral Scientist*, and *Explorations in Human Relations Training and Research*. He has contributed to the book *Innovations to Group Therapy* (Springfield, Ill., Charles C. Thomas, 1968).

Contents

THE FAMILY IN SEARCH OF A FUTURE

Introduction

Alternate Models for the American Family Structure:
Initiating Further Responsible Dialogue

There is much agreement today that American society is in transition, and considerable disagreement as to where this process may or should lead. Among the social frameworks seemingly caught on the crest of this wave of transition are the institutions of marriage and the family.

This is never more clear than when we examine our divorce statistics. It is safe to say that most men, women, and children in the United States have been touched by this experience, either in their own families or among friends and close acquaintances. One analyst has predicted that one-third to one-half of all marriages occurring this year are destined to end in a divorce court. I am reminded of a cartoon which recently appeared in the *New Yorker*: a young couple is shown leaving what is identified by a sign as the home of a justice of the peace. The bride, dressed in the latest "far-out" fashion, turns brightly to her young man and says, "Darling! Our first marriage!"

In part, this book is a result of my own experience with divorce. Throughout this painful process, I was struck by the fact that a large percentage of my colleagues (psychologists, psychiatrists, and social workers) either had undergone or were then undergoing a divorce. In the course of informal conversations, it became clear that even those professionals who considered themselves happily married were increasingly inclined to question the contemporary institutions of marriage and the family. I began to take informal notes, and in the course of two and a half years had more than sixty conversations with members of the helping professions concerning their marriages and divorces. Reviewing these notes, some main themes or threads could be distinguished:

1. With very few exceptions, divorce was as painful and as confusing an experience for these professionals as for any of their clientele.

Many psychotherapists reported remarks from their patients such as, "Doctor, if you can't make it, how can we?"

2. There was universal dissatisfaction with the divorce process, the legal complications and procedures, which were seen to be in great need of simplification and reform. Divorce, as an institution, was clearly recognized as being in need of regeneration. Many questioned alimony payments for wives able to support themselves or having private means.

3. Joking reference was often made to the fact that, not too long ago, man was thought to be naturally monogamous. The extensive divorce rate and the widespread practice of extra-marital affairs, in addition to the Kinsey Report and a host of contemporary studies, call into question the appropriateness of a monogamous relationship in which husband and wife depend exclusively upon each other for sexual satisfaction.

4. Many of the professionals interviewed noted that choices of mate are often made when the individual does not have the maturity and wisdom to make a good choice. Recognition of this fact has accelerated the acceptance of, and trend toward, plural marriages.

5. It was generally agreed that this society's expectations of marriage are such that they militate against the very existence of the institution in its present form. (See Hobbs, pages 30–31, for a succinct summary of these expectations.) Partners expect too much, and then are disappointed because their needs cannot be met. It was a common observation that people often seem to outgrow each other, or to grow apart despite their best efforts to the contrary.

6. There was a varied reaction to recent research which, in Reuben Hill's words, "Suggests that the advent of a child is not necessarily the fulfillment of marriage, but possibly the first point of cleavage that separates husband and wife—and that this cleavage widens with each additional child, disrupting the marriage relationship to such an extent that when the children are adolescents, the parents are so far apart that instead of being bereft at their leaving, they are, in fact, reunited, happy to pick up where they left off in the wonderful days before they had children." [1] Some professionals saw this process at work in their own marriage, others did not.

7. There were similarly varied reactions to Cuber's recent volume,

[1] For a popular summary of this recent research, see "The Most Unexpected Threat to a Good Marriage," *McCall's* (July, 1967), pp. 94 ff.

The Significant Americans,[2] a study which sought to examine whether men and women of achievement also tended to have outstanding sexual and emotional lives. (Cuber concluded that a large majority of these successful Americans tended to develop cool, detached, almost loveless marriages, possibly because this kind of relationship is so well adapted to the pursuit of a career.) While many professionals saw themselves as "family-oriented" rather than "career-oriented," there was some recognition that a demanding clinical practice or other career demands had interfered with a marriage.

8. Roughly 30 to 40 percent of the persons interviewed would agree with Cadwallader that, "Contemporary marriage is a wretched institution. It spells the end of voluntary affection, of love freely given and joyously received. Beautiful romances are transmuted into dull marriages; eventually the relationship becomes constricting, corrosive, grinding and destructive. The beautiful love affair becomes a bitter contract." [3] Surprisingly, however, more than 80 percent expected to remarry "within a reasonable time."

In questioning the institution of marriage, we question indirectly the whole area of man-woman relatedness and the nature and quality of contemporary relationships between the sexes. Perhaps one of the clearest indications of the deep separation between the sexes is evidenced by the pattern of seating arrangements at most lay and professional meetings. Women tend to sit together, as do men. What appears to be in operation here is a combination of estrangement, mild anxiety, and hostility; sex stereotypes [4] are clearly in full bloom. These elements are characteristic of most man-woman relationships today.

The strength of these forces (which create an attitudinal climate) can be gauged by the fact that the close relationship of marriage has not significantly affected the quality of estrangement existing between the sexes. Even in groups of married persons, women still seem to feel more comfortable clustering with other women and men more at ease with other men. To dismiss this phenomenon as merely a result of "similar

[2] Dr. John F. Cuber and Peggy B. Harroff (Mrs. Cuber), *The Significant Americans* (New York, Appleton-Century-Crofts, 1965).

[3] Mervyn Cadwallader, "Changing Social Mores," *Current* (February, 1967), p. 48.

[4] Herbert A. Otto, *Group Methods Designed to Actualize Human Potential* (Chicago, Ill., Achievement Motivation Systems, 1968), pp. 52–59.

interests" and "shared subcultures" indicates narrowed perception and a lack of sophistication.

A further index of the estrangement is that real friendship and understanding between the sexes is rare indeed. "Man" relates to "woman," and not to the individual behind the image he has built. Each gender is so blinded by the sex image of the opposite that the person behind the mask rarely emerges from the shadows. The two images relate to each other—the persons remain strangers.

It is possible that if we were to deal with the psychosocial roots of this estrangement (which, in part at least, is firmly anchored in the sexual self-image), this might have profound implications for the institutions of marriage and the family. As it is, artificial or superficial relationships constantly reinforce the estrangement between man and woman and its negative effect on the marital and family interaction.

For many decades the overwhelming weight of our research has been concentrated on marital and family dysfunction and disorganization. We have studied or sought to treat the sick marriage and the sick family without any clear conceptualization or theoretical framework for what we mean by a "healthy" marriage or a well-functioning family. Our efforts have focused on the pathology of the family, while neglecting family strengths. My own research in the area of family strengths[5] over the past eight years is a meager beginning; a massive effort in this area is needed to broaden our understanding of family and marital dynamics and the treatment of marital problems.

A major question implicit in the study of "healthy" families and marriages is: "To what extent does the American family structure

[5] Herbert A. Otto, "What Is a Strong Family?", *Marriage and Family Living*, Journal of the National Council on Family Relations, vol. 24, no. 1 (February, 1962), pp. 77–81; *idem*, "The Personal and Family Resource Development Programs—A Preliminary Report." *International Journal of Social Psychiatry*, vol. 8, no. 3 (Summer, 1962), pp. 185–195; *idem*, "The Family Resource Development Program: The Production of Criteria for Assessing Family Strengths," *Family Process*, vol. 2, no. 2 (September, 1963), pp. 329–339; *idem*, "Family Strengths in the Treatment Process: A Research Study." Monograph reporting project supported by the University of Utah Research Fund. *Canada's Mental Health*, vol. 14, no. 1 (January-February, 1966), pp. 1–6; *idem*, "The Minister and Family Strengths," *Pastoral Psychology*, vol. 17, no. 163 (April, 1966), pp. 21–28; *idem* and John Gabler, "Conceptualization of 'Family Strengths' in Family Life and Other Professional Literature," *Journal of Marriage and the Family*, Journal of the National Council on Family Relations, vol. 26, no. 2 (May, 1964), pp. 221–223.

contribute to the optimum development of the human potential of its members?" This is perhaps the key question for the assessment of any alternative structure. Certainly, the functionality of our major institutions can be assessed by asking, "To what extent is the institution contributing to the development, actualization, and fulfillment of human potential?" If we ask this question in relation to the school, the police department, the family, etc., it is crystal clear that our institutions are critically over-due for regeneration.[6]

As indicated by a spate of headlines, there appears to be some public readiness for such reformation of social institutions. To cite only two of these headlines: "ADVOCATES DIVORCE WITHOUT CHARGES—Divorce American Style should be granted without grounds, according to the President of the American Academy of Matrimonial Lawyers",[7] and "CATHOLIC SOCIOLOGIST URGES PROBATIONARY MARRIAGES." [8]

Compare the storms of indignation and the preaching from the pulpits which greeted the appearances both of Bertrand Russell's *Marriage and Morals* in 1929 and of Judge Lindsay's classic, *Companionate Marriage*, in 1937, with the almost casual acceptance of Margaret Mead's "Marriage in Two Steps," first published in a popular magazine in 1967. Is it possible that this lack of controversy and opposition represents a passive recognition that marriage and the family as social institutions are now seen as sufficiently dysfunctional as to merit a more objective assessment and, possibly, a regeneration? If this is the case, then certainly a responsible and widespread dialogue about alternate models is a vital part of this process and cannot be neglected. *Such dialogue might give further impetus to the development of programs designed to strengthen families, as well as encourage experimentation with new models.* It is now widely recognized that the average human being is functioning at a fraction of his potential. Perhaps we are also ready to recognize that the contemporary family is functioning at a fraction of its potential.

In this volume a number of nationally-known scientists respond to the proposal that alternate structures for the American family are a possibility and that further dialogue is a necessity at this time.

[6] Cf. John W. Gardner, *Self-Renewal* (New York, Harper & Row, 1963); and Herbert A. Otto, *Explorations in Human Potential* (St. Louis, Warren H. Green, 1968), pp. 408–411.

[7] Article, *The Chicago Sun-Times* (Sunday, October 29, 1967), p. 56.

[8] Article, *The Arizona Republic* (Phoenix, Saturday, March 11, 1967).

John F. Cuber examines the question, "Why consider alternatives?" and, from his perspective as a sociologist, concludes that we should accept "Pairings of the socially and physically mature . . . at any time at the mutual consent of the partners." He proposes a variety of domicile arrangements for the married pairs, including provisions for parents living separated both from each other and from their children, with the state assuming broader child-rearing responsibilities.

From a theological perspective, Edward C. Hobbs suggests a "dialogue-centered marriage . . . with sexual relationships not limited to the marriage bond . . . except that pregnancy-control would be utilized at all times . . . except when children are planned."

Sidney Jourard comments on underground experimentation with "Polygyny, polyandry, homosexual marriages, permanent and temporary associations . . ." and concludes that such experimentation should be legitimized and that marriage be "re-invented" as "serial polygamy to the same person."

"Marriage as a Non-Legal Voluntary Association" is proposed by Harold Greenwald, who suggests that, "If state registration were eliminated, people would stay together for the only reason that makes marriage really viable—because they wanted to."

Virginia Satir offers a series of new learnings and ideas which might improve all human relationships as part of her paper, "Marriage as a Human-Actualizing Contract." Although her paper was originally entitled "Marriage as a Statutory Five-Year Renewable Contract," it did not explicitly deal with this topic. Based on the title of her paper, the proposal that the marriage contract be renewable every five years was given considerable national publicity. At the 1968 annual meeting of the American Association for Humanistic Psychology, however, Virginia Satir pointed out that her original title was largely allegorical. The idea of the marriage contract as a periodically renewable legal bond remains a possibility which merits further exploration.

Ethel J. Alpenfels contends that hidden cultural values motivate human behavior and considers progressive monogamy (the practice of taking several partners, one at a time) as an alternative structure for the familial system.

Margaret Mead proposes two types of marriage, *individual* ("a licensed union in which two individuals would be committed to each other as long as they wished to remain together, but not as future parents") and *parental* (explicitly directed toward the founding of a family).

Albert Ellis examines the pros and cons of group marriage, concluding that it "seems very doubtful, however, that a great many people will rush into group marriage in the near future; it seems even more unlikely that this form of mating and family life will replace monogamy or polygamy on a world or even a national scale." Jealousy and interpersonal conflict in the group are some of the main reasons why Ellis believes group marriage faces great difficulties. Unfortunately, nowhere in his paper does Ellis make any reference to group dynamic techniques, or to the encounter group approach which, with the help of competent professionals, might go a long way toward resolving some of the problems inherent in a group marriage structure.

Gerhard Neubeck invites the reader to share with him a fantasy of a polygamous marriage. He concludes that "Only those who can deal effectively with complexity can make polygamy work for them."

Herbert Otto proposes the "New Marriage," which has as its main purpose the involvement of both partners in the adventure of actualizing each other's potential.

Joseph J. Downing, with a long-time interest in the hippy culture, offers "The Tribal Family and the Society of Awakening" as a viable alternative model.

Victor Kassel calls for polygyny after age sixty when ". . . there just are not enough men . . . Therefore, any man over age sixty could marry two, three, four, or five women over sixty."

Intimate networks of families, formed with the help of a professional, are suggested by Frederick H. Stoller, while Carl Levett believes that the absence of the father from contemporary homes calls for the parental presence of a trained professional "third parent."

Finally, George S. Rosenberg presents detailed background and analysis of "the implications of new models of the family for the aging population," citing a number of objections to a polygynous structure for the aged.

As is evident from this brief sampling, divergent viewpoints and perspectives have been presented. Each paper is highly individualistic and I have seen it as my function to seek clarification of style and English only where absolutely necessary. This is the fourth book which I have edited, and it was the most difficult to assemble. There were what appeared to be endless postponements of their deadlines by contributors and, with a few exceptions, delayed arrival of manuscripts was the rule. In one instance, the professional integrity of a contributor had to be questioned before a repeatedly-promised manuscript was forthcoming. It is my impression that these unusual difficulties are perhaps traceable in part to unconscious elements of resistance. Contributors may have unconsciously identified the volume as a threat to the existing family structure.

It was also of interest to note that a number of manuscripts contained a plea for a pluralistic approach. This is most appropriate, for we are a pluralistic society—with pluralistic needs. In this time of change and accelerated social evolution, we should encourage innovation and experimentation in the development of new forms of social and communal living.

A certain amount of experimentation with a variety of family structures has been conducted in communities (established primarily by young people) which have sprung up in all parts of the United States within the past five years. These organized living arrangements of couples and singles in homes, apartments, or on farms are variously known as utopian, intentional, or experimental communities. In my own research into experimental communities I have encountered a variety of cooperative living patterns, but so far no replication of the Israeli Kibbutz. I am inclined to agree with Stanley Diamond's statement that "the *Kibbutz* is not a folk society, it is not an extended family, or localized clan, nor is it in any way analogous to these." [9]

The establishment and decline of many experimental communities has been chronicled in the underground press (*Los Angeles Free Press*, *Berkeley Barb*, Chicago's *Seed*, New York's *East Village Other*, etc.), and in a journal called *The Utopian*, now in its third year of publication. To give the reader a clear idea of the experimental community movement, a document entitled "The Group Family," received from London, an article entitled "It's Just One Big Happy Family," from the *News of the World*, and an article entitled "Cold Mountain Farm," from the *Modern Utopian*, are placed in the appendix.

Although there has been considerable experimentation with dif-

---

[9] Stanley Diamond, "Kibbutz and Shtetl: the History of an Idea," *Social Problems*, vol. V, no. 2 (Fall, 1957), pp. 71–99.

ferent relationships and family forms within experimental communities, these communities have, almost without exception, been under pressure, harassment, and prosecution by police authorities and neighbors. Operating under such severe handicaps, aggravated by problems of space and of economic survival, the overwhelming majority of these communities can by no stretch of the imagination be considered adequate proving grounds for the testing and exploration of new relationship designs.

It is possible to invent and try out many models without hurting or destroying another person. Perhaps we need to recognize very clearly that the objective of *any model* is to provide both an atmosphere and a sustenance of loving, caring, and adventuring. This makes human growth, actualization, and unfoldment possible.

It is only with the advent of modern anthropological research and sociological theory that man has recognized his institutions, not as eternal verities, but as defined ways of being social. For the first time, he is now free to examine such institutions as marriage and the family with a certain amount of objectivity and to restructure these institutions, not in blind compliance to social pressures and economic sanctions, but in full consciousness of his needs and potentialities.

After five hundred thousand years of human history, man is now at a point where he can create marriage and family possibilities uniquely suited to his time, place, and situation. It is my suggestion that the "option to pluralism" offers a compelling challenge; namely, that we develop new forms of marriage and family which might conceivably add more warmth and intensity to human existence than we ever dreamed possible.

What will destroy us is not change, but our inability to change—both as individuals and as a social system. It is only by welcoming innovation, experimentation and change that a society based on man's capacity to love man can come into being.

JOHN F. CUBER

1

Alternate Models from the Perspective of Sociology

> *Freedom is the right to choose, the right to create for oneself the alternatives of choice. Without the possibility of choice and the exercise of choice, a man is not a man but a member, an instrument, a thing.*
>
> —THOMAS JEFFERSON

Sociologists have popularized the concept *ethnocentrism* but despite their ubiquitous cautions about its dangers, they often seem to have fallen into the same pit they admonish others to avoid. Probably nowhere is this tendency more prevalent than in their considerations of family structure and related institutions. The clear tendency is to accept the basic assumptions of the traditional religio-legal structure as almost eternal verities, subject only to a few modifications on the fringes and these often only belatedly, after the system itself has already manifested the changes.

The conventional stance is to describe the new modes, measure their incidence if possible, ascribe to them the term *deviant* and point out ways by which such behaviors can be "corrected" or "counteracted," suggesting that these are mere transgressions of the verities, not that they may herald the shape of better things to come. This static attitude often goes so far as to make many family sociologists appear to be not merely apologists for the *status quo* but apologists for a structural system already somewhat passé.[1]

---

[1] There are, and have been, a few for whom the above characterization would be inappropriate. Joseph Folsom, for example, in his well-known and respected books

The sociologist who gives much serious attention to anticipating social arrangements which might *replace* the current marriage-family-kinship system is suspect among many of his peers for his *avant garde*, if not downright subversive, intentions. At the same time, it is common-place, almost platitudinous in the genre, that all social forms are mutable and subject to constant change—even, upon occasion, revolutionary change—when their structures become incongruous with the realities imposed by other social systems, or when their own internal incongruities result in serious tensions or dilemmas. Just why the tacit exception is made of this one social structure has, to my knowledge, never been satisfactorily explained.

Why Consider Alternatives?

There are two somewhat separable foci for evaluating the suitability of a social system—its effect upon the well-being of the people on which it impinges, and the efficiency with which its collective goals are achieved. On either count an examination of the existing sex-marriage-family-kinship system as codified by law, ecclesiastical requirement, and popular platitude results in a negative appraisal. Increasing numbers of people are dissatisfied and unhappy with traditional roles and expecta-tions—and few consider that the goals of sex regulation and effective childrearing and socialization are satisfactorily achieved by today's system.

An illuminating heuristic device utilized by anthropologists for almost half a century may help to bring current circumstances in

---

on the family gave consideration and, for his time, sophisticated treatment of several alternatives and certainly was no apologist for the monolithic platitudes inherited from another era and repeated *ad nauseum* elsewhere. (For example, see his *The Family and Democratic Society*, New York, John Wiley & Sons, 1943.) Anthropolo-gist Margaret Mead has, upon many occasions, turned our attention sharply to the question of alternatives either implicitly by her references to other sex-marriage-family systems or by more direct confrontation with our own incongruous circum-stances. Barrington Moore, Jr., has effectively demonstrated how, by misuse of data, wrong inferences are drawn and significant innovations played down. (See his *Political Power and Social Theory*, copyright 1958, by the President and Fellows of Harvard College, parts reprinted as "Thoughts on the Future of the Family" in *Identity and Anxiety*, Maurice R. Stein, Arthur J. Vidich and David Manning White *eds.*, Glencoe, Ill., The Free Press, 1960.)

America into realistic relief. In a variety of respects people function in two separable and often contradictory spheres. One consists of a set of proscriptions concerning what behavior *ought* to occur and *why* it should follow the outline proscribed. This is variously called the "ideal culture," the "normative order," or simply the approved social code. The other, and often, but not necessarily, contradictory reality, consists of what *actually* occurs in concrete instances when overt behavior is observed. This level is referred to as the "real" culture, including the "norms of evasion," which terminology suggests that systematic contradictions to verbal expectations not only occur, but have a viability too.

Meanwhile, it is almost a platitude, at least since Freud, that individual well-being tends to be threatened when precepts, ideologies, and ideals which have been internalized are violated by the person himself, or by others who are significant to him. Just as unhappy is the condition of the social system when it must deal repeatedly with modal inconsistencies between its codifications and contrary conduct.

De jure and *de facto* are long-established concepts and are useful as analytic tools for examining the sex-marriage-family-kinship orders both in contemporary America and to a considerable extent elsewhere in the Western world. Somewhat typically, it will be found that there are discrepancies in varying degree and seriousness between the proscriptions for behavior and actual behavior. In stressing this lack of correspondence between the two, there is no assumption that any social system can necessarily set up behavior proscriptions which have universal acceptance under concrete circumstances—any more than individuals can always conduct themselves solely in accord with the role requirements directed by the system. The problem is, rather, one of degree, and the premise from which the following analysis stems is that when incongruities between preachment and practice pass a certain tolerance for deviation, the injuries done both to the society and to the individual legitimate re-evaluation.

The *de jure* system is codified in ecclesiastical and legal regulations varying only slightly among different religious groups and among the several states. It is manifestly clear that the following are the "oughts," the proper modes of thought and conduct. Monogamous marriage is the only accepted form with sexual behavior limited thereto; premarital unchastity and post-marital infidelity are clearly taboo. The nuclear family, consisting of parents and their children by birth or adoption, is not only a residential unit until the child achieves majority or is married, but is also an economic unit for consumption, mutual property holding and inheritance. Legitimacy is possible only where the parents are married at least by the time the child's birth is registered. Under certain circumstances the usual legal or civil ceremony to celebrate marriage may be bypassed, and a condition known as common law marriage recognized, which for most practical purposes is thereafter much the same as formal marriage. The expectation is that once entered into, a marriage ought to last for the lifetime of the spouses, although there is provision for presumably exceptional cases when this is not feasible. Under varying degrees of embarrassment and legal awkwardness, persons are permitted to divorce and, if they wish, to remarry. Marriages so ending are popularly regarded as having "failed"; the negative consequences for all parties concerned are given wide attention, the positive ones but little. The children of married pairs "belong" to them and only under the most extreme circumstances does the state or the church interfere in their socialization. It is the privilege of the adult pair, with varied regulation by state laws, to transmit their property before or after their deaths to their children and/or others largely as they choose.

Popular expectations compatible with the implications of the *de jure* system recognize a division of labor between the sexes, although certain deviations are allowed, to the general effect that women are the chief socializing agents, while the main function of the male is to provide the financial wherewithal for the maintenance of the enterprise. Between the lines of the legal and ecclesiastical proscriptions (and no less in the popular ones) there is an implication that in exchange for his support the man should secure monopolistic access to the wife sexually, and can assume that children born to her are biologically his, while the wife receives support for herself and her children and a status position in the community based upon her husband's accomplishments. While a kind of equalitarianism between the sexes is in some ways pretended, it is belied by innumerable facts, as well as fictions both legal and popular, which run through the whole fabric of ideology in the system—the husband is legally the "head" of the household; it is the male's obligation to "support" his children (even after divorce); the wife is supposed not only to handle the major responsibilities for small children, but is presumed to be superior at it; the employment of mothers outside their homes, while a growing practice, is still a minority condition; wage rates for males and females are rarely equal for the equivalent quality-quantity work accomplished. Parents are expected to "control" their children; children are expected to be obedient to their parents' wishes.

For any and all of the above there occur in the popular proscription system certain rationalizations for exceptions. Thus, under "certain circumstances" a married couple may be divorced with a minimum of disapproval; the unmarried may be unchaste (during engagement, men in the military services, etc.); mothers may be employed (husband's income is insufficient, there is a war, she has some important social skill or training, or, more rarely, she needs "self-expression.") But these are still rather reluctantly permitted; the monolithic nature of the *de jure* blueprint is almost everywhere asserted, and the parts of it are re-enforcing one to the other in innumerable logical ways.

As everyone knows, the *de facto* system has many characteristics which are in direct conflict with the *de jure* system, and while this is widely known it is very unevenly reacted to. Premarital chastity is now probably honored more in the breach than in the observance; post-marital infidelity is by no means rare, although there is an almost studied effort to play down its incidence and rarely, if ever, is it acknowledged that persons considered as one's own social equals really do such things. Growing amounts of child care and socialization are sub-contracted to a plethora of ever-expanding agencies as well as to make-shift arrangements. Many of these parent-surrogate institutions enjoy prestige status even though they seem motivated mainly by parents', and especially mothers', desires to escape many of the inconveniences of parenthood. (There is no intention here to assert, or even to hint, that these devices are necessarily deleterious to a child's optimal social and personality development; we are concerned only with the fact that they constitute contradictions to the formal ideology of the nuclear family.)

Further, the vast amount of deception, collusion, and pretense involved in the divorce process is probably so well known as hardly to need mentioning. The legal fictions and consequent collusion are mostly the result of archaic conceptions of sexual inequality and stereotyped assumptions about why spouses want marriages dissolved. There is practically no legal or even popular recognition of the rather simple fact that people wish divorces because they simply do not wish to be married to each other any longer. Such intentions must be camouflaged by well-established patterns of devious subterfuge, usually involving collusion between the adversaries and their legal representatives, including the court itself. The youth peer culture, although considerably varied between classes, regions, and other less rational categories, has reached a degree of autonomy which makes the legal and customary assumptions about parental control of children seem naive to the point of being ludicrous. Rare, indeed, is the parent who has any clear conviction that he does, or can, control many of his child's crucial activities or belief systems, although there is a studied reluctance on the part of many to acknowledge this openly. There are, of course, other contradictions between preachment and practice, but perhaps these are sufficient to point out that "the system" functions in a highly pluralistic set of alternative behavior modes while still under the umbrella of monolithic proscriptions.

To various degrees most knowledgeable people are aware of these and other contradictions between the *de jure* and the *de facto* orders in the sex-marriage-family-kinship system. The parting of the ways occurs when assessments begin. Well-ventilated "sides" line up in the perennial dialogue. One group looks to the eternal verities, sizes up reality (or at least that part of the iceberg which is apparent), and cries for a return to the ways of the fathers. The wringing of hands and pleas for return to history have been going on for a long time with little result, but the appeal apparently remains irresistible, at least for some. The second well-exposed group is more acquiescent; it considers itself broadminded, liberal, humanitarian, and tries to "understand" all these "deviances"— and even to rationalize them to a degree, by pointing out that "in the new world it's simply not possible to follow the old rules." Yet the implication is that it would somehow be better if we *did*. A third ideology is extant too. It holds mainly that the broad outline of the *de facto* system contains appropriate adaptations to the ideological and technological realities superimposed upon the sex-marriage-family-kinship system by the requirements of other interdependent systems, as well as by the tensions and incongruities within the sex-marriage-family-kinship system itself.

Consideration of Alternatives

It is from this latter position that, it seems to me, rational consideration of alternatives can well begin. Simply to endorse the emerging *de facto* orders is not enough. It is necessary to make evaluations, since it is not likely that all of the *de facto* beliefs and practices are necessarily conducive either to the efficiency of the system, or to individual optimal adjustment within it. The following outline, then, is not intended to totally replace the existent monolithic legal-ecclesiastical (and to some degree, popular) code, but merely to combine a series of alternatives for those whose sensibilities need a less restricted atmosphere for fulfillment and optimal creativity. In part it follows certain patterns already institutionalized in the *de facto* systems, and partly a series of projections beyond them, all interwoven to form what is offered as a rational, holistic, alternative order. Its features cannot possibly be equally palatable to everyone, although it will be found, I think to be a system with many choices built in.

A number of general ethical-social considerations and criteria should be met before the separate characteristics of an alternate system can be set forth:

1. The functional requisites devolving from a two-sex species and a dependent childhood must be met.

2. There should be no serious disruption of the overall basic values of the society, such as political and religious freedoms.

3. An alternate system should be a minimally-coercive system. Individuals and pairs should be allowed wider choices than the current *de jure* system grants, should be able to exercise these choices with greater freedom of conscience, and should be obliged to observe less concealment and pretense than is usually now the case. The supporting logic comes from assessment of the current situation in which countless persons of all ages suffer the consequences of having incompatible ideologies and restrictions imposed upon them. And society suffers the collective problems which follow from these personal dilemmas, resentments, and impasses.

4. Consequently, the proposed sex-marriage-family modes would be pluralistic, that is, not all married pairs, not all parent-child relationships, not all sexual conduct would be expected to be the same, since choices would be made variously among the alternatives offered. There would be built-in a recognition that there are many kinds of mentalities on the subject of marriage and sex, and child-rearing, much as there are many mentalities now extant regarding religion, esthetics, use of leisure, and political persuasion. That it takes a little doing to live among the various breeds should be obvious, but if we can learn to do with varied religions, leisure plans, styles of life, and political ideologies, why not also varied sex-marriage-family-kinship commitments and practices?

5. It is assumed, not without considerable research evidence, that optimal personality development and feelings of fulfillment occur when the patterns of expectation allow considerable choice, are open in the sense that deceit, subterfuge, and pretense are minimal, and democratic in the sense that one early acquires the expectation that the world is made up of a variety of human kinds. With coercion minimal, much of the need for rebellion and related adaptations is dissipated. All this does not mean, as will be seen later, that no restraints are imposed, but rather that the restraints minimize the need for schizophrenic-like reaction, now so often virtually required.

6. In formulating this pattern of alternatives the rest of the social system is accepted as given, even though it is acknowledged that alternatives exist there too. The present systems of quasi-democracy in political and social matters, inequalities of income and privilege, free choice of employment, public mass education, religious freedom, modified capitalism, and a fluid, dynamic occupational structure are all accepted as given. In accepting these there is no intention to endorse categorically everything we now have, but rather to recognize that since these currently *are* the systems, any sex-marriage-family-kinship system which pretends to be rational must be geared to them.

The conventional clichés about the family being the "basis of civilization" and order are already, of course, largely vacuous. Whatever may have once been a validation for such an assertion, surely today the dominance of the family over other social systems is very hard to document. Rather, it is obvious that the family is required to adapt to the needs of other institutions as expressed by selective service, corporation policies for relocating executives, success patterns in all the professions requiring high mobility, the scheduling of work hours for the convenience of the bureaucracy and not for the efficiency of family management, and so on. What the proposed system would offer to the larger society would be largely the consequence of having people free to carry out the various societal roles without the debilitations which presently plague so many personal lives.

The following, then, is a terse outline of a system of alternatives to which the above logic seems to lead. There is no particular significance to the order since, being a system, one can start anywhere with the description.

An Alternative System

1. Pairings of the socially and physically mature (maturity to be defined, but certainly somewhere in the "teens") would be permitted at any time at the mutual consent of the partners. These pairings would presumably exist for general sociability and might or might not include sexual activity, but in any case, at the discretion of the pair. Whenever such pairs should desire to make public acknowledgment of their relationship, probably called "marriage," they would be free to do so with any kind of religious or civil ceremonies they might desire.

Prior to marriage or in the absence of it, couples would be expected to practice contraception and would be expected to limit their childbearing to the married stage. Contraceptive programs would be state supported and sponsored. No suppositions are made regarding the permanence of marriage, but the pair having children would be presumed to be responsible for the maintenance of their children whether remaining married or subsequently dissolving the marriage, much the same as is now the case, with the exception that state facilities for child care would be available and, hopefully, on a less niggardly basis than now. Termination of marriage would be at mutual consent and, as now, professional service would be available for those individuals who would feel that assistance before or after divorce might be helpful.

It is recognized that the dissolution of pairings by mutual consent really means in practice dissolution whenever *either* wishes dissolution. This is a hard fact of human association, regardless of fiat. It is now accepted for termination of friendships and of engagements and in a pragmatic sense is true of marriages too. A legal status can be enforced from the outside, but a psychological one cannot. Thus, it would be expected that in this system, as currently, there would be considerable numbers of rejectees, people whose performance in the pair was simply not up to the other's expectations. Expectations under this system, however, would be more realistic than now, for an individual would know that maintenance of the pair was a function of mutual gratification and not a duty which a frustrated mate was obliged to perform. I think it not unrealistic to anticipate, however, that a general recognition of the removal of the present legally-sustained crutches might have a salutary effect both upon the attitudes toward relationships and the attitudes toward the mate himself.

2. Married pairs could maintain any of a variety of domicile arrangements. Something resembling the present nuclear family would, of course, be permitted but not regulated. The pair might live separately from one another or together and separately from their children. Whatever course chosen, however, would necessarily impose responsibilities and could be changed if and when so desired. Since the responsibility for rearing and socializing children would be shared by parents and state, there would need to be provisions for more institutional and state participation in the socialization process.

3. It follows from the foregoing that such a fluid system would make no impositions regarding the sexual conduct of persons married or unmarried. If pairs wish to be monogamous, "selectively promiscuous" as Ellis has suggested, or celibate, it would be up to them. Similarly with respect to such options as homosexuality or traditionally "deviant" sexual practices.

Such a system would separate interdependencies which in an earlier era were linked together in traditional marriage. Sociability between the sexes, sexual conduct *per se*, reproduction, child-rearing and child-socialization could (any or all) be pursued independently of the others the various alternative combinations could now be on a rational basis because effective contraception has essentially separated reproduction and sexual relationship. Adoption has separated reproduction and child-rearing both for the natural mother and the adoptive parents; parent-surrogate systems separate reproduction and child care and management; the employment of women makes possible maternal financial responsibility to children with or without marriage. At present, any such practices, with the exception of contraception among married pairs, must undergo a gauntlet of practical difficulties and attitudes of inappropriateness and unacceptability. In the alternative system, while there would still be practical problems, they would be easier to solve because the system would allow for them; eventually there would be less stigma and feelings of inappropriateness. Provisions in the new system would work in the direction of translating our cultural know-how into practical choice.

4. Necessary legal changes would involve the removal of present-day restrictions and/or a lessening of the amount of regulation imposed upon people who wish to follow less "conventional" modes. Other legal

changes would be needed in the areas of taxes, inheritance, establishment of paternity and consequent responsibility, and the combined state and individual responsibility for socializing and rearing children.

Evaluation of Alternatives

These alternatives are not so much visionary as they are simple projections of *de facto* trends and, perhaps more importantly, legitimations of deviations which today are accepted either grudgingly or not at all. These alternatives, as we have already said, presuppose no radical change in other social systems, such as political "democracy," inequalities in income and privilege, mass public education, religious freedom, modified capitalism, and fluid occupational structure. To a considerable extent these changes would simply be tardy recognition of several *de facto* modes which are now known to exist but have the tenuous status of "norms of evasion," that is, enforcement is weak or sporadic, and punishment is token.

This whole pattern of alternatives is seen as incorporating a number of considerations which are considered to be positive.

1. *De facto* innovations in a social system, particularly when long-standing and growing, deserve legitimation, unless it can be *demonstrated* (not merely asserted) that they are destructive of the system.

2. The anachronisms, hypocrisies, injustices and uncertainties which at present are known to plague many people, and which are disruptive of optimal social functioning, as well as of happiness and mental efficiency, would be removed or at least largely reduced. Any sensitive individual conversant with the realities of the man-woman world which stem from the incongruities between preachment and practice, and between naive (but sincere) expectation and subsequent (but realistic) disillusionment, would stand to gain immeasurably through the establishment of a system in which intentions, expectations, and realizations could come more nearly into congruence.

3. The alternative system provides an atmosphere more conducive to several freedoms—freedom of mate choice, sexual expression, voluntary parenthood, occupational freedom for woman and the resultant emergence of total personality for her, as combined state and individual responsibility for child-rearing would free her for more varied, socially useful, activities.

4. In a certain sense, it could be argued that this pattern of alternatives is simply a logical extension of many of the basic values of American society anyway, a *laissez-faire* acceptance of what the *avant garde* is already doing, with the important difference that adaptive choices would now have a legitimate rather than an illegitimate status and their practitioners would be free of present potentials for embarrassment and possibly severe social sanctions. This, of course, is the system's strongest claim for viability—that it incorporates and somewhat extends practices already extant, and perhaps increasing, in an environment which is now in many ways hostile, while at the same time conducive to such practices. In other words, the new system is a clarification process.

There is no assumption, however, that this is a panacea. Specifically, it is expected that there will be some people who are irresponsible even when their responsibilities are as minimal as this system presupposes. It is, however, contended that there ought to be less irresponsibility because fewer persons would find themselves in the kind of entrapped conditions (e.g., inability to get a divorce) as is now the case. Nor would the system preclude the possibility of sexual exploitation any more than the present one does. Yet many of the present reasons for exploitation, such as the appeal of the furtive and clandestine, would be somewhat minimized. Moreover, some people would still be poor—too poor to take care of their children; some kind of public assistance would probably still be necessary. There would still be children born out of "marriage" despite the expectations, but with the general recognition that sexuality is normal. With greater availability of the pill, or possibly some better technology, this problem should be markedly reduced. The overriding faith is that an open system reduces the motivation for duplicity and deception and that improved self-concepts would result from a closer correspondence between behavioral proscriptions and conduct.

Nor is there the naive expectation that this new establishment would or should come quickly, although efforts to hasten it would seem to be in order. Nor is it assumed that there would not be maladapted individuals once such a new system were legally authorized. Just as in political and religious spheres, it would be expected that we would still have our familial fundamentalists, mentalities which for whatever reasons, intellectual or otherwise, prefer ideological orientations from some past era. There is, however, nothing in this proposal which would preclude their maintenance of such forms; they would be denied, however, what they now tend to assume, namely, some special prerogative to interfere with the lives of others. Like the justifications for political, religious, and other cultural pluralisms, the thrust of the argument would be that these alternatives are essentially democratic and, in the broadest sense of the word, also Christian.

EDWARD C. HOBBS

2

An Alternate Model
from a Theological Perspective

The greatest risk run by an essay written on this topic by a theologian is a persistent and pervasive misunderstanding of what theology is, what a theologian does, and therefore what "a theological perspective" means.

The popular view of theology is that it consists of a systematic organization of the beliefs of some religion or religious group; if this be the case, there can be no such thing as an *alternate* model for the family structure, but only the already-well-known variety of models (or variations on a single model) endorsed by current religious groups.

But, in fact, theology as such is not the exposition of a collection of beliefs or of a body of doctrines, even though "historical theologians"— that is, those whose research is in the history of theological formulation —do something very like this; their work, however, is no more contemporary theology than the work of historians of science is contemporary scientific research. Nor is theology the attempt to rationalize beliefs which are already held without proof, though some particular theologies may indeed give such an impression.

Instead, *theology is the "languaging" of that understanding which is implicit in faith.* Another way of putting it would be to say that *theology is the clarification of the "God"-function in a given community of faith.* Each of these definitions requires some explanation, since the key terms are used as ambiguously as the term "theology."

"Faith" is used here in its primitive Christian sense, not in the sense of blind belief, nor in the sense of "*The* Faith," but in its original meaning as *the commitment of one's future to X,* a commitment *made by response to whatever encounter requires decision and action.* Since all human beings encounter such situations with some frequency, and must make one sort of response or another, everyone lives by faith, in this sense of the term. The major difference between one faith and another would be *that* for the sake of which, or in terms of which, one makes the response—or, put slightly differently, the difference would be a difference of "X's" to which one commits one's future.

We have used the term "X" for the deciding factor in a situation which presents possibilities or options—whether that factor be an end or goal, a value, a style, an ideal, or whatever—to avoid using an all-too-readily misunderstood term. But now it can be revealed that in the ancient world the usual term for what we have called "X" was "God."

Since there are obviously many different factors in terms of which our responses to possibilities are made, it is important to emphasize that "X" is the *deciding* factor, or ultimate factor, in terms of which all other factors are evaluated. Even so, there are many of such deciding or ultimate factors (what Tillich liked to call "ultimate concerns") which means that there presumably would have been many "gods" in the ancient world—and, were the term still in such use today, many gods today. This is just the case; the multitude of gods was generally recognized in the ancient world, even though adherents of any particular one may have looked down on the gods of others, denying on occasion their power and even their liveliness. (One's own God was always—almost by definition—the best, the most powerful, the most "living" God.)

An over-simplified summary might be as follows: *Human response (hence decision and action) to what is encountered in life is in terms of some deciding or ultimate factor to which, in effect, one commits one's future in such response.* This is (in ancient language) the act of faith in one's particular God. Implicit in such "faith" in a "god" is an *understanding*—a mode of relationship to one's existence, or a way of being-in-the-world. This *understanding* can be languaged (brought to expression in language) and thus clarified, elucidated or explicated; such languaging is the task of theology.

Even within a given community of faith (such as the Christian one, from which standpoint the present chapter is written) there will be wide variations in theological expression which are both possible and legitimate. Not only will available languages vary (both in the common linguistic sense, such as Greek and English, and in the "conceptuality" sense, such as Gnostic and existentialist [1]) but also the contexts within

---

[1] For an extended discussion of this point, see my article, "Recognition of Conceptuality as a Hermeneutical Tool," in *Texte und Untersuchungen zur Geschichte der altchristlichen Literatur*, Band 88 (Berlin, Akademie-Verlag, 1964), pp. 464–477.

which responses are made. Even in the face of a single situation, and in response to a single "god" or determinant-of-concern, there might well be alternative actions taken, and thus different expressions in language.

Marriage from the Perspective of Christian Tradition

The only controlling factor of a given community's theological expression will be its ultimate commitment, or its God; all other factors in a given situation may vary. In the case of marriage, this is quite evident within the historical period of the Bible.

The Hebrew patriarchs had several wives, in some cases begetting offspring (considered legitimate heirs and members of the family) by their wives' maids—who were presented to them for that purpose by the wives themselves (Abraham, *Genesis* 16:1–6; Jacob, *Genesis* 30:1–13). In *Deuteronomy* 21:15–17 it is assumed that a man may well have two wives. King David had several wives (*2 Samuel* 5:13), in addition to the (at least) six he already had in Hebron before moving to Jerusalem; his son Solomon had seven hundred (!) who were princesses, not to mention three hundred concubines (*1 Kings* 11:3). (Even if this figure is legendary, it indicates the acceptability of such harems; the criticism leveled at Solomon by the Biblical author is not the number of his wives, but that they turned him away to worship foreign gods.) In the event of a man dying without offspring, his brother was to beget children by the widow, offspring who would be regarded as children of the deceased (so-called "levirate marriage," *Deuteronomy* 25:5–10).

Although monogamy seems implied by many other laws in the Old Testament, and presupposed on the whole by the authors of the New Testament, many variations in marriage-structure are exhibited. Jesus attacked the then-current legal structure for divorce, which permitted men to divorce their wives with great ease and callousness (probably on grounds of the inhumanity of such treatment of women, though it takes the form of an exegetical argument); the evangelist Mark, living under Roman (not Jewish) law which permitted women to initiate divorce, added the further clause that it was also wrong for women to divorce their husbands! (*Mark* 10:2–12; notice that Jesus could not have spoken vs. 12, since it refers to a situation non-existent in Palestinian Judaism.

Paul recommended celibacy most highly in view of the impending end of this world, while permitting marriage as non-sinful, though second-best (*1 Corinthians* 7:25–28, 32–34). In Corinth the church was proud of the fact that one member was living (sexually) with his father's wife (stepmother?), thus exhibiting his Christian freedom from the Law. (Paul angrily attacked the practice; but it was at least once attempted, even if mistakenly, as a proper form of expression of Christian faith.) It is also possible that in the church at Corinth a form of "virginal marriage" was practiced, whereby a couple "married" but agreed to have no sexual relationship; Paul considered this too heavy a demand on human powers of restraint, and recommended that sexual abstinence be restricted to short periods in the case of married persons (if, in fact, he is referring to such a practice at all).

In the case of marriage, then, as in all other cases, theology cannot simply repeat past formulations, customs, traditions, and practices as evidence of what must be now and forevermore. There is not only precedent for constantly new attempts to language the responses and relationships called forth by present situations and possibilities, but a real necessity for it, if theology is to be anything other than a repeating tape-recording of the once-vital theology of the past.

The demands laid upon theology in each new situation are primarily these: 1. *Fidelity to the activity/relationship* ("faith") *and to the locus of worthwhileness or meaningfulness* ("God") *which give rise to such languaging;* 2. *Attentiveness to the changing context(s) within which faith acts,* i.e., to the culture and the specific situations in which we live; 3. *Care and precision in its choice and use of an appropriate language in which to clarify the understanding implicit in the activity and relationship called faith.* (This last point has been central in the discussions of hermeneutics during recent decades, but it has become extremely acute since the recognition that the keystone of the entire linguistic structure of theology, namely "God," has dropped from meaningful usage in contemporary culture. Thus, the task of theology—at least as far as its meaningfulness and utility for the general public is concerned—has been rendered difficult in the extreme. It is almost as though "energy" and all synonyms for the word had become meaningless in general usage, and a physicist were trying to write a popular treatment of his field for mass consumption. The task is not impossible—one hopes!— but it is at least problematic.)

It is with all three of these demands in mind that we proceed to consider what an alternative model for the American family structure might be, from the perspective of theology—in our case, Christian theology.

Christian Theology as a Background for an Alternate Model

The changing context within which theology must function today is, at least in American culture, one of increasing dissatisfaction with the present institution of marriage, a dissatisfaction both cause and result of the increasing failure of particular marriages. At the same time, there is a continued determination to maintain some semblance of the family structure which has hitherto served as the primary means of establishing the relationship of children to society. The major new factor in this context is the development of relatively secure means of controlling pregnancy.

The rapid rise in the divorce rate is only one aspect of the dissatisfaction with marriage; an increase in non-permanent, extra-legal marriage-like liaisons among college-age youth is another. Yet, even with the increase in the divorce rate, American society seems to be intent on preserving a family or family-like situation for the children involved. While there is still the ideal of lifelong monogamous marriage, combined with an ideal of permanent and stable family-structure within which children may mature healthily and happily, it is striking that in practice we work much more vigorously toward bringing about the second idea than the first—or, at least, we do so insofar as legal and social pressures may be brought to bear on the matter.

It seems probable that much of present-day dissatisfaction with marriage stems from a tension between the desire to provide a stable family-structure for the rearing of children and the desire to achieve satisfying and meaningful relationships with the opposite sex at many levels. Prior to the development of secure means of pregnancy-control, there was not much alternative to the combination as we have developed it in Western culture: sexual relationships usually resulted in the production of children, for whom a family-situation was urgently required; hence marriage combined the features of both sexual regulation and family structure.

Without pregnancy-control, it might still be possible to maintain a stable family-structure for the rearing of children while leaving considerable freedom in intersexual relationships to the husband and wife provided the husband did not have strong feelings about actual physiological paternity of his legal offspring (i.e., the children of his legal wife, whoever the actual father might be). In fact, many primitive peoples take just such an attitude, even when they are aware of the physiological connection between sex and procreation. But in our culture this has not been the case; many men find adoption of children emotionally impossible, and apparently many more find artificial insemination of their wives (in the case of the husband's sterility) difficult to accept. The "tie of blood" is still felt to be paramount in paternity, in the mass of the population.

The tension between two aims in marriage—sexual relationship and child-rearing—has probably been aggravated in the modern period by the rise of emphasis on romantic love as a basis for marriage. This tends to become selection in terms of the sexual aims, which all-too-often do not coincide with family-and-children aims. When mate-selection is largely in terms of suitability for establishing and maintaining a family, dissatisfaction with the sexual-relationship aspect is not usually sufficient cause for disruption of the marriage by divorce, especially when other outlets are possible; but if the marriage fails to prove adequate in terms of family-needs, disruption of the family-unit is not so serious a catastrophe, as the disruption is happening to an already-inadequate structure. Though this might be taken as an argument for return to parental selection of marriage partners, or perhaps an "advance" to computer-selection, neither alternative is likely to commend itself in our day as a happy solution to our dilemma!

The tension between sexual relationship and child-rearing has also been aggravated by an increase in leisure time among the general population. A marriage in which the couple rarely have time to see each other because of work-responsibilities, or in which extended relaxation and comfort for the couple's social and sexual relationships are almost non-existent, is not so likely to show evidences of dissatisfaction as a marriage where the couple have leisure for extensive and profound relationships. Again, the solution is surely not to eliminate leisure! Rather, leisure tends to serve the function of laying bare the inadequacies of relationships more rapidly and significantly than would be otherwise the case.

It is quite possible—indeed, it seems highly probable—that we have come in our time and culture to lay demands on marriage of a kind and to an extent which it cannot often fulfil. If marriage is "the institution whereby men and women are joined in a special kind of social and legal dependence, for the purpose of founding and maintaining a family" (Webster's *New International Dictionary*, both Second and Third Editions), it has also become the institution whereby men and women are expected to find their sole sexual relationships, their primary or sole partners-in-dialogue, their primary valuation and appreciation as persons, and the fulfilment of their romantic aspirations or longings. No doubt there are many happy coincidences of fulfillment of all these expectations in a single relationship; few would dare to claim, however, that this is the case in any significant proportion of American marriages. It is still the dream, but it is close to being the impossible dream for most marriages.

Yet there is hardly any alternative to marriage as a basis for the family unit. If this is the case, it should be seriously questioned whether the demands might not be lessened or altered in some way that could provide for a greater possibility of fulfillment and satisfaction of the needs which we have hitherto brought to marriage, without losing the family-structure itself. Further, the form of the question for us here is *whether Christian theology itself might not provide some clues as to possible directions such modification might take.* While it is possible to treat theology as though it justified perpetuating the past and its forms (of marriage, as of everything else), we have already seen that this is an erroneous understanding of theology; indeed, if theology is rightly understood, *it should be expected to take the lead in proposing constantly-new modes of expressing the understanding implicit in its relationship to what happens.* (That this rarely occurs is more a judgment on the irresponsibility of theologians than a failure of the public to understand rightly their role.)

If this is the context within which faith acts and theology must function with respect to the question of marriage and family structure, we must next consider briefly what would constitute fidelity to that particular "faith" in that particular "God" in terms of which Christan theology carries out its task. At this point the risk of caricature through over-simplification is so great as to suggest abandonment of the attempt; to state this both concisely, on one hand, and with care and precision, on the other, has always either eluded theologians or caused their formulations to be labeled heresy (or worse, "popularizations" and "slogans").

Nevertheless, the purpose of this chapter cannot be attained without some sort of statement as to the controlling "understanding" in relation to which this proposal is made, and in terms of which it must be judged, insofar as it claims to be "theological."

The ancient language, which itself was shorthand for fuller explications, called this understanding "The God and Father of Jesus Christ," meaning "that which Jesus Christ acknowledged as his God, and called Father." Slightly more fully, it spoke of its God as Christ, Father, and Holy Spirit (literally, "breath"). This particular language was used in response to the situations and encounters in which human beings were compelled to respond; the language itself was not the primary response, but only a languaging of the response. The three sub-varieties of God-language in the classical formulations of "Trinity" referred to three "masks" (Latin: *persona*; Greek: *prosopon*) worn by the chief "actor" in the drama of life (i.e., "God"), who, or which was, what might be referred to in other "faiths" as "Fate," or "Chance," or "Luck" (whose Latin name, *Fortuna*, still survives in our speech, as in fortunate, unfortunate, fortune, etc.), or "Devil," or (more vaguely) "Reality," or "the way it goes." The three "roles" or "masks" ("persons" is a mistranslation) may be oversimply identified as particular responses and relationships to three kinds of encounters or situations: (1) *exposure of the self;* (2) *contingency or limitation;* and (3) *need of others for our aid.*

The responses and relationships to these encounters or situations were: (1) in the face of the situation which *exposed or revealed the discrepancy* between one's pretensions and one's actual life-as-lived, one responded with acknowledgment of the true situation and a "change of understanding" (Greek: *metanoia*, poorly translated "repentance"); (2) in the face of the situation which confronted one with the *contingency or limitation* of his existence, one responded with creative thankfulness for the new—albeit in many cases unwanted and limited—possibilities presented by the limiting situation itself; (3) in the face of the *encounter with others in their need for help*, one responded with action directed to the benefit or good of those others.

That is, (1) *the exposure of inauthenticity* ("Judge") was responded to as healing ("Savior"), or liberating from bondage to the past ("sin"); the one who brought about judgment and salvation in the ancient Hebrew world was oiled or anointed, hence known as "the oiled one," (Hebrew: *Messiah*; Greek: *Christ*); (2) *the limiting situation or encounter* (discovering one's "creatureliness," or meeting the "Creator") was responded to as possibility-offering, as new-good-bringing (as a "Father" treats his children), as to a loving Father whose gifts are not always what was desired or even understood, but as presenting good possibilities nonetheless. (The coming of Santa Claus is a scarcely-disguised form of this: the old man with a long white beard who lives way up there, to whom requests are sent, who brings good gifts to all the children of the world, though not always what was requested and usually more expensive ones to the children in wealthy homes; about whom the great lie is that he only brings gifts to good children, so "be good for goodness' sale"); and (3) *the situation of encounter with others in their need* was responded to as relationship-offering, or community-creating; the other becomes one's brother through the act of "loving" him, i.e., ministering to his need. (This was the "Life-breath"—*spiritus* in Latin—of the "body" or community of men; such a usage survives in the French *esprit de corps*, literally "spirit of the body.")

Even further simplified, this God-language might be called a mode of expressing a "Yes-response" to all of the encounters and situations of life. To respond with affirmation to exposure of my inauthenticity, to limitation, and to need-of-others-for-me, was to discover in them myself, my father, and my brother. Christian faith might be called the responsive and active relationship to all of the encounters of life which is confidence that they always and unfailingly offer possibilities for good, or for "life"—that is, for value, or worth, for creativity, for purpose, or for whatever constitutes "life" for men.

Or, it might be formulated as an affirmation that all human existence including the unknown and not-quite-manipulable future, is trustworthy, rewarding our trust with worth. But these oversimplifications must be considered in the light of the triple-formulation, or triple-role-character, presented above, for it clarifies just what kind of "Yes" or "trust" is implied in the various kinds of situations or encounters of human existence.

Probably the most important form of the theological questions concerning marriage and family structure is the *ethical*. Here theology is constantly confronted with the danger of failure to meet the second demand laid upon it, the demand for attentiveness to the changing context(s) within which faith acts. When an adequate and appropriate response to a given type of situation is found, and it is given language by theology, there is an overwhelming tendency to assume that the matter is settled once and for always; such formulations become the "law" for Christians. In view of the insistent claim in the New Testament that *Christian faith means freedom from the law, in precisely this sense of law*, such a retrogression in our understanding can be seen as infidelity to the fundamental commitment involved in Christianity. Nevertheless, since context, cultural and situational, tend to change slowly for the most part, it is all too easy to justify this reliance on past solutions, and Christian theology often ends by wearing the garments of the lawgiver—a strange role for those whose roots are in a radical freedom from law!

Once more, the warning must be given that radical compression of what Christian ethics involves risks distortion; such a risk must be taken, however, if we are to consider the issue at all. With this caveat, let us note that the initial ethical question occurs in the third kind of situation or encounter, the meeting of the third "mask" of God, namely, the encounter with others in their need. The briefest way of stating this understanding is in the so-called "great commandment," that we love others as ourselves. The "Golden Rule" is simply a variant on this formulation, as is Kant's "categorical imperative." It is in terms of this way of being present to ourselves and to others that all Christian ethics must be discussed. Observe that the formulation is not an arbitrary demand, for it is rooted in the understanding that *in my neighbor's need is the possibility for my own "life" or "health"* (Latin: *salvatio*, hence English "salvation"), for responding to him in love means meeting the life-giving breath ("Spirit") of the body of which we are "members" or organs, namely the body of mankind. Observe also that the formulation does not tell us *how* we are to love our neighbor (who is interpreted as anyone we encounter in need of us—the Greek word for "neighbor" is *heteros*, which simply means "other"), but only *that* we must do so, if we are to find life; the means of doing so is left to our own wisdom and understanding, frail though they may be.

Observe, too, that this does not say we are to love our neighbor *instead of* ourselves, but only *as* ourselves, which also implies that I am to love myself—not hate myself, not make a suffering doormat of myself, but love myself, and extend this same love to my neighbor, who is not just the one close to me, not just my friend or family, but whomever I might meet who has need of my love. Love means, above all, to act for the sake of the other, to act for the good of the one to be loved.

For the Good Samaritan to love the man lying in the ditch (*Luke*

10:25–37) meant to stop to aid him, to bind up his wounds, to convey him to the hospital, and to pay his hospital bills; it did not mean to emote over him, to feel affectionate toward him (they were, in fact, enemies), nor in fact to feel *any* special way about him. To love myself means, to act for my own good and welfare; to love another means to act for his benefit, good, and welfare, and to meet his need of me.

The two major complications of what might otherwise be a clear-cut matter are these: (1) We are not always really sure of just what the other's good really is, or sure of just how to achieve what we understand that good to be; (2) there is not actually just one neighbor; there are many, and many needs confront us, meaning there are many to love, often more than we could possibly manage (indeed, isn't one point to saying we should love not only our friends and family, but our enemies as well, that we must consider many needs and goods, not just one?).

The nearest solution to the first complication is to do our best to gain the wisdom, understanding, and knowledge needful for the task of loving others, though again there are limitations to this. (I cannot become expert in medicine, and economics, and politics, and anthropology, and psychology, and mathematics, and what-have-you, though my various neighbors' needs may involve all of these.) The second complication may have no solution except our honest efforts to see what needs we can in fact meet, which we have the capability of meeting, which are most urgent, and so on. Were we to advance a formulation which settled a hierarchy of meeting needs, we would once more have submitted to "law" instead of the freedom we have been given to love others, in ever-new and ever-changing situations, often without adequate precedent or guide. The recognition of the "rule-of-thumb" or "generalized-guide" character of most of the items of the "religious codes" frees one to ask afresh as to the most appropriate means of loving one's neighbor as oneself.

By this point, it must be evident that from a theological perspective there can be no justification for continued insistence on the forms of marriage and structure we have inherited, at least not simply because we have inherited them. It would be quite possible to meet the demands of Christian theology and Christian ethics with other structures, though not with just any structure; the criteria for such new structures would be those we laid upon theology itself earlier in this chapter. It is in the light of this framework that the following alternative model is suggested for marriage and family structure in contemporary American society.

Inadequacy of the Current Model

Marriage is "the institution whereby men and women are joined in a special kind of social and legal dependence, for the purpose of founding and maintaining a family;" in our culture this special kind of social dependence is taken to include an exclusive sexual relationship. Economic relationships vary from state to state, and almost all other aspects of the dependence vary also; even the permanence of the bond is understood in vastly different ways, as the laws of Nevada and New York on the subject at once reveal. In addition to the "founding and maintaining a family" dimension of marriage (the essential dimension, without which we would be discussing another subject), sexuality is almost invariably understood as the other dimension. Additional dimensions are desired and wished for, but we generally regard any serious expectation that *all* the others will also be found in a particular marriage as idealistic if not naive. Now, there is no doubt that, given the attitude toward paternity felt in our culture, there has really been little alternative to the model of marriage and family we have inherited. The family consists of father, mother, and their own children (except in such cases of necessity as sterility or other impediment to begetting or conceiving offspring, or the adoption of children whose natural parents for some reason cannot provide them with a family); children are produced by sexual intercourse, and *vice versa*—that is, intercourse produced children frequently, and such production outside the marriage-bond resulted in familyless children, or children born into a family whose "father" was not the actual father of such children. In the light of the resultant problems, it was natural to make the sexual relationship exclusive to marriage, and a necessity within it (so that consummation was a necessity for a valid marriage and impotence, for example, sufficient impediment for annulment). There would really not seem to be much basis for understanding marriage otherwise (even polygamy does not alter this aspect of our marriage model, for the family unit is still related intimately by physiological paternity), provided always we retain our strong feelings about natural paternity and its decisive importance to the family unit.

But the recent development of highly effective (and, presumably, completely effective before long) means of pregnancy-control spells an end to this necessary connection. To be sure, unless artificial insemination with the husband as donor became widely practiced, there would still be the necessity of *some* sexual relationship between husband and wife—sufficient to result in the desired offspring—but the *exclusive* sexual arrangement between husband and wife as we know it would no longer be required by the need of founding and maintaining a family.

On the other hand, it can be rather cogently argued that *permanence* of the marriage relationship *is* intimately connected with the quality of the family structure as a matrix for the maturation of children. Probably it is better to have no marriage than a bad marriage, as far as the growth of children is involved, and better to have a series of marriages than no marriage at all; still, a permanent family unit offers a stability which is highly desirable for the healthy rearing of children. Yet it is this very feature of American marriage (still proclaimed as the intent of every marriage, and still thought of as the only proper attitude toward marriage, but long-since given up as a universally expected pattern) which is the first to be abandoned, in favor either of fatherless or motherless family units, or of a kind of serial-polygamy through divorce and remarriage.

Thus, we are in the process of abandoning the permanence of marriage, while maintaining (in law and in principle, even if less in reality than ever before) *its sexual exclusiveness.* We may seriously ask whether something approaching a reversal of these two attitudes toward marriage might not promote a healthier and happier model for American family structure. At least we must ask whether it might not be possible to find a model which would respond to the needs of the children in the family structure, in terms of their greatest good, and at the same time provide for a greater good for the parents than seems to be experienced under the present model. (This is to invoke the principle of love as a basis of judgment upon any model.)

If we may once more indulge in vast over-simplification, let us inquire as to features probably making for stability and permanence, due to mutual satisfaction, in the marriage relationship, since such features ought to be sought in any model we might propose. In addition to sexual satisfaction (which rarely is sufficient, in the absence of other kinds of satisfaction, to support a stable marriage, and whose exclusive connection with marriage we propose severing), we would probably include mutual interests of some sort, compatibility of personalities, mutual liking or affection, perhaps mutual appreciation or esteem, and

some degree of fulfillment of all these mutualities through language—
that is, an ability and a willingness to *dialogue with each other*. In fact, it
seems highly probable to this theologian that genuine mutuality hinges
on some degree of openness to one another, an openness which because
of our humanness must find expression in language, and thus fulfil
itself in dialogue if possible. (The prejudice of a professional whose field
is language might readily be suspect here; and it cannot be denied
outright. But if we are to see humanness as intimately bound up in
language, and the "linguisticality" (horrid translation of Heidegger's
Sprachlichkeit) of human existence as the horizon of all our understanding and relationships, we must inevitably place a very high premium on the place of language among human beings. And since human
beings are fundamentally social, not lone individuals, then this language
must aim at being dialogue.

It may be objected that human mutuality and openness find their
highest expression in sexual intercourse, not in linguistic intercourse or
dialogue. But unless one is determined to preserve a traditional institution at all costs, or to maintain a theory of how things ought to be rather
than how they actually are, we can easily discern the fallacy of such a
view of sex. The ease with which men have accepted prostitution (nay,
created it!), and with which many women take it up and live with such
a casual-encounter style of sexual relationship, is alone adequate to
suggest that great intimacy is not required, or even induced, by sexual
relationship. The millions of marriages which fail in American society,
which nevertheless have included constant sexual relationship, also attest
to the failure of sexuality to provide intimacy. The revelation of actual
sexual activities in American men and women by the Kinsey reports,
further reinforced by the more recent studies by Gebhard, also suggests
that great intimacy is not necessarily associated with sexual relationships.

Of course, human sexual relations *may*, and often do, result in great
intimacy; but so do many other forms of human intercourse. Even eating
meals together may have such a result, and while not limited to two
persons, as sexual relations commonly are, meals often become
occasions for development of close ties among persons.

And while sexual intercourse finds much greater meaning and value
when it is engaged in by persons who are also open and intimate with
each other in non-sexual spheres, and tends to reinforce such openness
and intimacy *if it exists*, it is also true that many other kinds of relationships or intercourse likewise are enhanced by, and in turn enhance,

openness and intimacy. In fact, it may be that we have tended to romanticize the meaning of the sexual experience, primarily in order to hedge it in further to married couples only, and to warn of the dangers of illicit sex for those not married to each other. This is not intended in any way to imply that the sexual experience is less than a wonderful one, an exciting one, and a meaningful one. But it is possible for it to be all of these and still not restricted to a single pair of people who engage in it exclusively with each other, for life, in combination with the commitment to raise a family together, hold property and income in common, and so forth. Our tendency in this culture is to praise sexual relationship, and immediately to warn, "But watch out! It leads to serious consequences, of which you must beware!" The consequence we really mean is pregnancy, but the one we increasingly name is intimacy, since in an era of successful pregnancy-control, the former warning falls on ears that know better.

It might also be recalled that sexuality is shared with most animals, and in the case of mammals, a sexuality very similar indeed to our own; but we do not share language with them, by means of which we interpret and re-interpret all our experiences, including sexuality. Are we prepared to claim great intimacy and openness (of a bovine sort) between bull and heifer because of this sexual relationship? Language is distinctively human; sexual intercourse is not.

Proposed Model for Family Structure

The outline of this model for the American family structure, as an alternative to the model we have inherited from out past, is already apparent to the reader. It may be summed up in the following manner:

Marriage would be, as in all societies, the institution whereby men and women are joined for the purpose of founding and maintaining a family; the special kind of dependence, however, would be limited to reproduction of offspring by the couple. Sexual relationships would not be limited to the marriage bond in any special way whatever, except of course that pregnancy-control would be utilized at all times outside the marriage, and always within it except when children are planned as a result. The primary kind of attraction between the couple, and the primary basis upon which their relationship would be founded and developed, would be centered upon the matter of *dialogue and openness*, a willingness or even eagerness to share oneself—ultimately to the greatest possible extent—with the other person, to expose oneself and one's needs and concerns, and to accept the other self and its needs and concerns.

In a sense, the question would be more "With whom would I be willing to converse and share everything for the rest of my life?" than "With whom would I most enjoy sex for the rest of my life?" which tends to be one major hidden question under the present arrangement. Marriage would be a lifetime bond, broken only with great difficulty and for great cause, once children were present or on the way, since this is the purpose of such a model; the likelihood of success under such a system would certainly be vastly greater than under the present one, particularly if the urges and drives of sexual connection were not irrevocable and exclusively tied to the marriage. A *dialogue-centered marriage* would not only offer much greater chance of stability, but would probably offer a much healthier and more satisfying framework for the nurture and growth of children, which is one of the primary aims of marriage as an institution.

Dialogue may be regarded as *love in language*, since it hinges on mutuality, on loving the other as oneself, if it is to succeed; hence, it especially meets the theological criterion we considered earlier. Sex may or may not involve love; orgasm occurs whether one seeks the good of the other or not, although it is more gratifying to normal persons if one does seek the other's good as well as one's own. But *dialogue* simply cannot happen without love. *Openness* may occur without it, as is seen in any psychoanalysis (where the analyst does not reciprocate by exposing himself to the client); dialogue, however, demands mutual and reciprocal seeking for the other's good and the common good.

Dialogue and openness in language further enhance the possibility of responding to the exposure of the discrepancy between one's pretensions and one's behavior, in such a way as to find acceptance and transformation of one's understanding of oneself (i.e., of responding to the judgment as saving, or to the "Judge" as "Savior," sometimes called "faith in Christ"); since acknowledgment of one's true situation and behavior is vital to any change in these (unless I can see myself as an alcoholic, for example, I can see no need to change from what I am and do with respect to alcohol), a relationship which provides a ready possibility of accepting but also honest discourse will offer much benefit. It is hard to see how a merely satisfactory sexual relationship would aid in such self-acknowledgment and change of direction. Thus we have found a special advantage in this model from the first as well as the third modes of encounter or situation, called "masks" (*personae*) of God. It is possible to show a connection also with the second, and thus round out the case, but that connection is less obvious, requiring further special discussion, and is hardly worth the space required here, for purposes of this proposal.

It is quite possible, perhaps even probable, that as time passed in a marriage along the lines of this model, the sexual relationships of the couple would be increasingly or even wholly located within the marriage relationship. This would probably be the line of least resistance, as well as more satisfying, as the couple came to know each other more and more intimately. *But since sexual attraction would not need to be a significant factor in such marriages, and thus in fact might not be very high in any particular one, it would be important to maintain the right to freedom on this point.* Otherwise, the model would degenerate in practice to the present one, without the added advantage the present arrangement often possesses in this one respect, namely, an initial sexual attractiveness between the couple in most cases.

Whether such a model would find general support is doubtful. All alternative models would meet the inertia which society exhibits in such matters; this one would meet the added hazard of attack by theologians of conservative stamp on grounds other than those here adopted. Rejection of the model on the basis of the kind of demands laid on theology in this chapter would be legitimate, provided the inadequacy of this model or the superiority of another were shown. But in theology, as in every field, inertia reigns; only remarkable forces overcome it sufficiently that new answers to old questions, or even new questions, may be acceptable before they too become irrelevant.

The ground for hope, however, also is to be found in the data of theology; for the clearest point of all is that the future may be trusted, and that it accepts us, provided we are ready and willing to respond repentantly, creatively, and lovingly to the surprising and unexpected novelty it brings.

And this would suggest that we need not be pessimists on this question. After all, there was Jesus, and Paul, and Luther, and John XXIII. And Galileo. . . .

SIDNEY M. JOURARD

3

Reinventing Marriage:
The Perspective of a Psychologist[1]

One man, one woman and no, or some, children, all living together in a household separate from others—this is the pattern, or better, the cliché, of marriage and family life that has evolved in the Western, industrialized world.

If this design evolved as an economic necessity, as the most efficient way for people to live in order to keep the economy going, and the social structure with its power elite unchanged, the design has been successful. In fact, throughout history people at the top have seldom lived the same pattern of marriage and family life as have the larger, working majority. The rich and aristocratic have invented ways to live that have scandalized the majority as much as they have evoked envy. The conventional marriage, while preserving the *status quo*, has failed to serve such important functions as facilitating personal growth and self-actualization in the married couple and their children. In fact, I see compulsive adherence to conventional definitions of husband-and-wife roles or son-and-daughter roles as a factor in disease.[2] Entrapment in forms of interaction that merely preserve a system imposes stress on those who are trapped, saps them of zest and morale, and contributes to illness.

As a psychotherapist, I have often been called upon to do "marriage counseling," and I have been struck by the incredible lack of artistry and

---

[1] This chapter is based on some extemporaneous remarks I made as a discussant at the Symposium. I have not attempted to present an authoritative paper, but rather to encourage further exploration and inventiveness in the ossified field of marriage and family life.

[2] See my book, *The Transparent Self* (Princeton, Van Nostrand, 1964), especially chapters 6, 9, and 15, for discussions of the sick-making potentialities of various family and occupational roles.

creativity in marriage partners. Either person may be imaginative in making money or decorating a house, but when it comes to altering the design for their relationship, it is as if both imaginations had burnt out. For years, spouses go to sleep night after night, with their relationship patterned one way, a way that perhaps satisfies neither—too close, too distant, boring or suffocating—and on awakening the next morning, they reinvent their relationship *in the same way*. There is nothing sacred to the wife about the last way she decorated her house; as soon as it begins to pall, she shuffles things around until the new décor pleases her. But the way she and her husband interact will persist for years unchallenged and unchanged, long after it has ceased to engender delight, zest or growth.

I have similarly been impressed with the same lack of creativity in inventing and reinventing oneself. A man can retire and, if one sees him asleep, his facial expression changes, the chronic neuromuscular patterns which define his "character"[3] all dissolve, and he is unconscious for a few hours. On awakening, it is as if a button has been pushed; his facial musculature reproduces the mask that defines his physiognomy, he holds his body as he did yesterday, and he behaves toward everyone he encounters as he did yesterday. Yet, in principle, he has the possibility of recreating himself at every moment of his waking life. It is difficult but possible to reinvent one's identity, because man is human, the embodiment of freedom; his body and his situation are raw material out of which a way to *be* can be created, just as a sculptor creates forms out of clay or steel. The medium imposes limitations, but the sculptor has many degrees of freedom to create forms, limited only by the extent of his imagination, his courage, and his mastery of technique. The sculptor confronts a heap of clay, imagines a possible form that will be pleasing and meaningful to him, then sets about transmuting this image into a structure that can be *perceived*.[4] He may create and then destroy dozens of approximations of his image, until finally he hits upon the

[3] Wilhelm Reich has discussed "character" in terms of neuromuscular patterning; significantly enough, he speaks of both character- *and* muscular-armor. See Reich, *Character Analysis* (New York, Orgone Institute Press, 1948).

[4] My existentialist bias is showing here, as rightly it should. See S. M. Jourard, *Disclosing Man to Himself* (Princeton, Van Nostrand, 1968, especially chapter 14) for a discussion of creativity that applies as much to the creation of self and of relationships as it does to such productions as a painting, a symphony, a dance or a sculpture.

form that "works." But that same sculptor, confronted by the "clay" of his being and the being of his wife, can neither imagine nor make new ways for him and her to interact that please, that fulfil needs and values other than the visible *form* of their relationship.

It is both possible and difficult to reinvent a relationship. The difficulty has to do with barriers to change that exist in persons and in the environment. If I begin to change my ways of being myself, I feel strange: I feel I am not myself. The different ways of being may make me anxious or guilty. And so I may revert back to familiar, but stultifying, ways of being myself. If I persist in my efforts to reinvent myself, and begin to behave before others in new ways, they may become angered or affrighted. They don't recognize me. And they may punish me in any way at their disposal for changing a part of *their* world— namely myself—without first "clearing it" with them. Much invaluable growth and change in persons has been invalidated and destroyed by the untoward reactions of well-intentioned others. Perhaps it is because if I change a part of their world, the part that I embody, there is an invitation or demand presented to them to change *their* ways of being. They may not be ready or willing to change their ways. If I lack "ontological security," [5] I may withdraw my changed being from their gaze, wipe out the new version of myself and, in a moment of cowardice, reproduce the being I used to be. I then become an impersonation of a past identity.

When one is involved in a relationship like marriage, the difficulty in reinventing the relationship is compounded because there are two persons, two imaginations, and two sets of needs to be considered; two sets of change-possibilities are involved. But it is still possible for two people of good will to discuss images of possibility, reconcile differences that arise, and then set about trying to actualize themselves. It is possible to play games with a relationship, to experiment with new forms, until a viable way is evolved./What seems to thwart this kind of interpersonal creativity is failure in imagination on the part of either partner, dread of external criticism and sanctions, and dread of change in oneself.

One barrier to change in any institutional form is economic. People have to make a living, and they must find a way to interact with others which facilitates, or at least will not interfere with, the necessities of producing goods and maintaining the social, political and economic *status quo*. Societies that are under external threat and societies that have

[5] Cf. R. D. Laing, *The Divided Self* (London, Tavistock, 1960).

an insecure economic base are "one-dimensional" [6] societies. Their techniques for socializing the young and for social control of adults are powerful, and incontestable. Deviation from the norm is severely censured, by necessity, because the security of the whole society is endangered.

But in America, the most affluent nation that ever existed, objective reasons for enforcing conformity are diminishing. At last, we have the power and the wealth (despite protestations from conservative alarmists to the contrary) to ground *a fantastically pluralistic society*. Indeed, *not* to capitalize on our increased release from economic necessity, *not* to "play" creatively with such existential forms as marriage, family life, schooling, leisure pursuits, etc., is a kind of madness, a dread of, and escape from, freedom and the terror it engenders. Forms of family life that were relevant in rural frontier days, or in earlier urban life, that mediated compulsive productivity and produced a mighty industrial complex and immense wealth, are obsolete today. I think that our divorce rate and the refusal of many hippies, artists, and intellectuals to live the middle-class model for marriage and family life attests to this obsolescence. There exists, in fact, in this nation a great diversity of man-woman, parent-child relationships; only the middle-class design is legitimized. The other patterns, serial polygamy or communal living where the nuclear family is less strong, are viewed with alarm and scorn by the vast, conforming majority. These patterns exist as a kind of underground. But both the myriad ways for living married that are secretly being explored by consenting adults in this society, and the designs that have existed since time immemorial in foreign and "primitive" societies, represent a storehouse of tested possibilities available to those who would experiment with marriage. Polygyny, polyandry, homosexual marriages, permanent and temporary associations, anything that has been tried in any time and place represents a possible mode for existential exploration by men and women who dare to try some new design when the conventional pattern has died for them. *Not to legitimize such experimentation and exploration is to make life in our society unlivable for an increasing proportion of the population.*

If it is sane and appropriate for people to explore viable ways for men and women and children to live together so that life is maximally

---

[6] Cf. H. Marcuse, *One-Dimensional Man* (London, Routledge & Kegal Paul, 1964).

potentiated, then we must ask why it is not being done with more vigor, more openness, and more public interest. We must wonder why divorce laws are so strict, why alimony regulations are so punitive, and why people experience the end of one way of being married as so catastrophic that they may commit suicide or murder rather than invent new forms or patterns of life.

I suppose it is the task of sociologists to answer this question. But from both a clinical and existential point of view, something can be done.

I have encouraged couples who find themselves in a dead marriage but still find it meaningful to live together, to begin a series of experiments in their ways of relating. The image or metaphor that underlies this experimentation is the view of *serial polygamy to the same person.* I conjure up the image of two people who marry when they are young, who live a way of relating that gratifies needs and fulfills meaning up to the point of an impasse. One partner or the other finds continuation in that way intolerable. The marriage, in its legal form, is usually dissolved at this point. But it is also possible that the couple may struggle with the impasse, and evolve a new marriage with each other, one that incudes change, yet preserves some of the old pattern that remains viable. This is their second marriage to each other.

The end of the first can be likened to a divorce, without benefit of the courts. The new marriage, whatever form it takes, will also reach its end. It may last as a viable form for five days or five years, but if both parties are growing people, it must reach its end. There is then a period of estrangement, a period of experimentation, and a remarriage in a new way—and so on for as long as continued association with that same spouse *remains meaningful for both partners.* Any one of these marriages may look peculiar to an outsider. For example, one marriage of perhaps seven months may take the form of separate domiciles, or weekend visits, or communication through the mails or by telephone. But the idea is that, for growing people, each marriage is, as it were, to a new partner anyway. So long as both partners are growing, they have had a polygamous relationship. The "new" spouse is simply the old spouse grown in some new dimensions.

This model of serial polygamy with the "same" spouse must be viewed as only one of the myriad possibilities for persons who desire marriages to try. The cultural storehouse can also be drawn upon for other models. We could even envision a new profession, that of "marriage-inventor," who would develop and catalogue new ways for men and women to cohabit and raise children, so that no one would be at a loss for new forms to try when the old forms have deadened and become deadly. It is curious to me that college courses and textbooks on marriage all turn out to be propaganda for the prevailing cliché of marriage for the middle class.

I could invent a course that might be called "Experimental Marriage," complete with laboratory. The laboratory would consist of households where every conceivable way for men, women, and children to live together would be studied and tested for its viability, its consequences for physical and mental health of the participants, its economic basis, etc. If the prevailing ways of marriage are outmoded, if men find it necessary to live with women or with somebody, on an intimate basis, and if children need parents, then experimentation is called for to make more forms of cohabitation available, on an acceptable basis, for everybody. The present design is clearly not for everyone.

There is an implication here for those counselors and therapists who engage in marriage- and divorce-counseling. Elsewhere [7] I have discussed the politics of psychotherapy: Is the therapist committed to the social *status quo*, or to a more pluralistic society? *If to the former, he then functions as an agent of socialization, a trainer of persons so they might better "adjust" to the* status quo. *If to the latter, he is more akin to a guru, or existential guide.* If he follows the latter model, then he will indeed function as a marriage counselor in ways different from his more conventional colleagues. He will encourage people who find themselves in marital impasses to explore new ways; he will be able to help his client invent a new way of being married to someone, rather than persuade him to perpetuate the conventional marriage form with his present partner in despair, or with a new partner in unfounded hope.

The inventive counselor of spouses or entire families, as I say, does not aim toward fitting human beings to a marital design that was invented by no one for no particular human beings. Rather, he is more akin to a consultant to artists whose creativity has dried up as they pursue tasks of vital concern to them. If Picasso, or Gilbert and Sullivan, ran out of ideas, or the courage to produce them in action, we might hope that they would have available to them a consultant who

---

[7] S. M. Jourard, *Disclosing Man to Himself* (*op. cit.*).

would help them turn their imaginations on again, and inspire them with the courage to produce what they imagined.

Since each man, woman, and child is a potentially creative artist in the invention of family roles, the marriage and family counselor should certainly be no less than a family-invention consultant. It happens that everyone is the artist-of-himself, whether he is reflectively aware of this or not. He is responsible for what he creates out of what he has already become. But the banality of self-creation that we see everywhere attests to alienation of each from his self-creative powers. The stereotypy of family relationships in a society with an economic base that enables and requires creative diversity further attests to this alienation. A good therapist brings his patient back into contact with his powers. A good family counselor awakens his clients to the experience of their freedom or powers, and to their responsibility to reinvent their situation.

Concretely, this way of being a counselor requires that the counselor himself be more enlightened than his clients regarding barriers to inventing or changing patterns of life. It helps if he is himself continuously engaged in inventing and reinventing his own interpersonal life, so that he is, and exemplifies, a vital and growing person. His imagination and knowledge can then draw upon a repository of family life possibilities larger than that possessed by his clients. The criterion of a successful solution to marital and family-relationship problems is not the *appearance* of the relationship, but rather *the experience of freedom, confirmation, and growth* on the part of the participants. Thus, "seeking" spouses can be encouraged to try such things as: living apart from time to time; lending their children to foster parents for a while; trying to be radically honest with one another, etc. So long as the counselor is not himself existentially or professionally committed to one image of family life, he can encourage spouses to explore any and all possibilities, the criterion of their success being, not "saving the marriage" in its present form, but rather a richer, fuller experience of growing existence and honest relationship.

The group structure most effective for fighting an enemy is an army with its platoons and regiments. The group structure most effective for providing care and training to infants, as well as companionship, love, and sex for the adults, is the now-outmoded family structure. The family structure for the emerging age of affluence and leisure cannot be prescribed or described in advance—only invented.

4

Marriage as a
Non-Legal Voluntary Association

One of the major criticisms increasingly, and I believe appropriately, directed at clinicians has been the tendency on the part of many to accept present-day institutions as sacrosanct and to see their primary task as consisting of adjusting the "deviant" individual to the society in which he finds himself.[1] At a time when our country is experiencing unparalleled affluence, cities torn apart by civil strife, and the dedication of hundreds of thousands of young men to the establishment of a democracy in Saigon with the aid of napalm, defoliation, and the bombing of civilian populations, many consider their sole duty to be one of helping patients to function smoothly and adequately no matter how unpalatable the institutions within which they are enmeshed.

Nowhere is the unquestioning and uncritical acceptance of the *status quo* more startling than in the field of marriage and the family.[2] While the modern family has been indicted as the cause of schizophrenia,[3] neurosis,[4] psychomatic complaints,[5] and even murder, there is almost no mention of changing the institution; instead, there is a vast proliferation of research, effort, and literature devoted in some way to modifying the

[1] Robert Coles, "Doppelganger for Freud," *The New York Times Book Review* (October 8, 1967), p. 8.

[2] Hyman Spotnitz and Lucy Freeman, *The Wandering Husband* (Englewood Cliffs, N.J., Prentice-Hall, 1964).

[3] Murray Bowen, *The Origin and Development of Schizophrenia in the Family*, a paper delivered at Forest Hospital, Des Plaines, Ill., May 24, 1961.

[4] Nathan W. Ackerman, *The Psychodynamics of Family Life* (New York, Basic Books, 1958).

[5] Therese Benedek, "The Psychosomatic Implication of the Primary Unit," *American Journal of Orthopsychiatry*, vol. 19 (1949), pp. 624–654.

individuals or their interaction in order to make marriage, as presently constituted, workable. For example, in an excellent collection of papers entitled *The Psychotherapies of Marital Disharmony*,[6] there is no mention of changing the institution of marriage itself although Ackerman points out that "the social institution of marriage is not working as we should like it to" (p. 153).

Reference to alternate forms of marriage is significant only by its absence. There is, for example, no mention of Judge Ben Lindsey or his suggested companionate marriage. Yet it may be much more to the point to change the institution, or at least make it more flexible, than to force the individual into its procrustean bed. And many a marital bed is procrustean indeed.

Sexual mores have undergone a considerable change within our recent past. Certainly the Kinsey reports have documented these changes.[7] In fact, their very publication and wide dissemination, as well as the more recent publication of Master's and Johnson's study on the human sexual response, would have been impossible only a few decades ago.[8]

In the last twenty years of my practice I have been impressed by these striking changes in sexual mores. The incidence of virginity in unmarried women over the age of twenty-five has diminished almost to the zero point. Today, some therapists of my acquaintance look upon such belated retention of the hymen as deviant and are as puzzled by such behavior as were the members of one of my therapy groups when a twenty-eight-year-old belly dancer announced that she was still a virgin. Of course, woman's right to sexual satisfaction and sexual experimentation is now as accepted in many enlightened circles as her right to vote. Certainly our definition of female promiscuity has changed; now a woman who can count her premarital affairs on the fingers of one hand often considers herself deprived.

The most striking change, however, has been the increased tolerance for, and open discussion of, such deviant sexual practices as

---

[6] Bernard L. Greene, *The Psychotherapies of Marital Disharmony* (New York, The Free Press, 1965).

[7] Kinsey *et al.*, *Sexual Behavior in the Human Female* (Philadelphia, W. B. Saunders, 1953).

[8] William H. Masters and Virginia E. Johnson. *The Human Sexual Response* (Boston, Little, Brown & Co., 1966).

homosexuality, wife-swapping, and group sex. In fact, some of these practices have become so institutionalized that there are special journals devoted to making such adventures easy to arrange through the use of their classified advertising.

The attitude which seems to be evolving among certain enlightened groups is that sex practices between or among consenting adults are no longer the concern of anyone but the individuals involved. Indeed, there is increasing pressure for the repeal of existing restrictive legislation, much of which is *de facto* repealed by non-enforcement. For example, although adultery is against the law in New York State, there are practically no prosecutions under this law—despite the fact that until recently divorce was granted only on these grounds; the courts, therefore, were constantly apprised of adulterous actions.

In suggesting that marriage may be a non-legal voluntary association, I am not insisting that this be the only form of marriage. Increasingly, we are becoming a pluralistic society and many individuals within our society may perhaps need other forms than state-sanctioned and state-enforced monogamy.

There are many reasons that may be advanced for the continuation of marriage in its present legal form. Marriage is needed for the protection of the children that may issue from such a union. Marriage is needed for the protection of women who could not obtain the balm of alimony were they rejected by an ungrateful husband. Marriage and the family are necessary for the stability of our society and our way of life. Marriage is important for dealing with community property and to regularize income and other taxes.

Is state-regulated and state-registered marriage necessary for the carrying-out of all these functions? Certainly the most important single humane objection to voluntary association is its possible ill-effects on children. Here one might point out that safeguards already exist and that a father's responsibility for the support of his children does not depend upon his being married to their mother, nor is his being married an iron-clad proof of his fatherhood. In addition, there now exist many more economic opportunities for women, as well as state and federal aid (inadequate though it may be) when the father is unwilling or unable to support his children. There is no guarantee that the properly married husband will, by the mere fact of having his marriage attested to by the state, be any more willing or able to support his children.

The other problem that children of marriages not hallowed by the state present is the so-called psychological stigma of their parenthood. Let it be clear that I am not suggesting non-marriage, merely that state certification of such marriages is not always a *sine qua non*. I know of no child whose friends demand that he produce his parents' properly-executed marriage certificate before accepting him as a playmate.

The protection for the woman which state-regulated marriage is said to provide is often more illusory than realistic. In actuality, many thousands of husbands (and an increasing number of wives) annually desert their spouses despite the sanctity of both governmental and religious marriage services. Perhaps such a non-legal voluntary association would severely cut down on alimony payments. However, an increasing number of women are becoming disenchanted with the institution of alimony, as maintaining economic and often negative emotional ties with a man they would well be rid of. When alimony payments are substantial, they often have the practical effect of preventing the woman from forming a permanent relationship with a new partner within the bonds of legal matrimony. Even the newly-created organization dedicated to women's rights called the National Organization of Women (NOW) implies that it is dissatisfied with the present-day alimony system. It would be equitable for the female partner to expect some division of economic assets as in the dissolution of any partnership.

As far as the stability of the family is concerned, there is much evidence that state-witnessed marriage is becoming more ineffectual all the time. The great increase in geographic mobility and the drafting of large numbers of young husbands have contributed greatly to the precariousness of marriage. The enormous increase in divorce and separation rates in this century are significant indices of this decreased stability.

Where substantial property rights are involved, independent agreements are usually entered into by the parties to legal marriage. There is nothing to preclude such agreements being made by the parties in a voluntary association. The same can apply to tax situations, with the slight modification of the definition of marriage from state registration to voluntary assumption of the status.

I have tried to deal with some of the objections to marriage as a non-legal voluntary association, but I am sure there are other problems for which solutions would have to be found. What then are some of the advantages of taking marriage out of the sphere of legalism?

First, there would be the elimination of the nonsense of most divorce proceedings. For example, until this year the only legal ground for divorce in New York State was adultery. In those rare cases where the testimony was not arranged by perjury or collusion, the mechanics of spying and catching the mate in the act of committing adultery was an obscene, not to mention inhuman, act designed to cause considerable anguish and emotional difficulties to mates and children alike. Such divorce laws seem to be calculated to be of assistance to few. Cooling-off periods, compulsory marital counseling, and other similar procedures seem to show remarkably small records of success. Strangely enough, what would seem to be the most logical reason for divorce, the marital dissatisfaction of both partners, is rarely if ever explicitly accepted as a bona fide reason for divorce in the United States.

If state registration were eliminated, people would stay together for the only reason that makes marriage really viable—because they wanted to. How can marriage be fulfilling to mates or children when it is maintained by legal fiat, not by the desires of the partners to the relationship?

Perhaps persons so impulsive that they would dissolve a fundamentally sound marriage due to momentary pique need the protection of cumbersome and outdated legal machinery, but this is hardly reason enough to enchain the rest in matrimonial relationships which may no longer be desirable or functional.

Furthermore, legal bonds do not by any means insure the continuity of a marriage. For those who can afford it, divorce or annulment offer no special difficulty except the emotional ones mentioned. For those who cannot afford it, there is always separation or desertion. Fundamentally, then, marriage in the sense of living together is already essentially a voluntary relationship. Many young people have chosen non-legal voluntary associations and a recent issue of *Esquire* magazine contains photographs of three such couples, all undergraduates, who were brave enough to proclaim to the world that they are indeed living in voluntary association. In a recent radio interview, one of the *Esquire* editors stated that in researching the story he had found a great many couples who had chosen similarly.

Much of the opposition to such marriages comes from representatives of organized religion. Actually it would seem to me that by rendering marriage unto the state, religious bodies have actually surrendered an important segment of religious freedom. The orthodox Jewish religion has provision for a religious divorce. Similarly, the Roman Catholic religion has provision for a church-granted annulment.

Neither of these are recognized by the state, and anyone who would rely on such religious procedures and remarry would be considered guilty of bigamy. True freedom of religion should permit religious bodies to make their own regulation for effectuation and dissolution of the marital state. Those who prefer religious marriage should then be free to follow the dictates of their consciences.

Changing marriage to a free voluntary association would also permit experimentation in varieties of family life which would possibly be more in keeping with the needs of many individuals for whom life-long monogamous marriage is unsuitable. Perhaps many would find that polygamy, polyandry, and group or tribal marriage were more compatible forms for them. Certainly *de facto* faithful monogamy, as the Kinsey investigators have established, is far from universal.

Those who wish it should certainly be permitted to continue to seek the alleged security of state-certified marriage; others not so inclined should similarly be permitted and encouraged to try alternate forms. There is need for serious study of the comparative satisfactions of legal and non-legal marriage.

Seeing marriage as a non-legal voluntary association requires some confidence in the image of man—as one who can establish fulfilling relationships through choice, not coercion.

5

Marriage as a
Human-Actualizing Contract

When I was asked to write this paper, the idea excited me. I have many thoughts about this subject. As I sit down now to write, I am overwhelmed at the enormity of their implications. My power of imagination fails me in visualizing how all these changes could be accomplished, given this world as it is today, with its vast numbers of people and the prevailing low image of a human being; this world, where love and trust are rarities and suspicion and hate are expected.

Person-person, male-female, and adult-child relations, as they exist today, seem pretty inhuman and many times even anti-human. The current legal and social structure frequently acts to aid and abet these inhuman contacts. Given the state of human relations today, it is not hard to understand current human behavior in marriage, the family, and other human transactions.

The effect of these inhuman and anti-human relations seems abundantly obvious in the widespread presence of mistrust and fear between human beings. If relationships are experienced as mistrust and fear, how can love and trust come about? Statistics on alcoholism, drug addiction, suicide, murder, mental illness, and crimes against persons or property are more specific indications of inhuman and anti-human treatment. Continuing wars between nations, racial strife, and poverty are global evidences of these same practices.

While these statistics do not include every person in our population, enough are included to make it more than just a random or accidental occurrence. This raises the basic question: *Is this how man really is inherently or is this the result of how he has been taught?* I would have to stop this paper right now if I believed that man's present behavior is the result of what he is, inherently. I believe man's behavior reflects what he has learned and I take hope in the fact that anything that has been learned can be unlearned and new learning can be introduced.

This, of course, raises another basic question: *What are these new learnings?* To talk about a change in the marriage relationship without talking about making changes in the human beings who make the marriage is, in my opinion, putting the cart before the horse. I would like to present some ideas which might go a long way toward moving us all a notch forward in our whole human existence and consequently in the marriage relationship.

What Would Happen If:

1. *Children were conceived only by mature adults?* If these parents felt prepared and knew, beyond few questions of doubt, that they had the skills to be wise, patient, and joyful teachers of human beings, of creative, loving, curious, real persons? Further, if this conception were an active mutual choice representing a welcome addition, instead of a potential deprivation or a substitute for a marital disappointment?

2. *Parenting were seen as probably the most crucial, challenging, and interesting job for each adult engaged in it?*

a. The business and the working world would manage in such a way that young fathers would not be asked to be gone from Monday to Friday. Men are essential; their non-presence hands child-rearing almost exclusively over to women. This skews the kind of parenting a child gets, which is reflected in his image of himself and others. An integrated person needs to have an intimate, real familiarity with both sexes. For many children, fathers are ghosts, benign or malevolent. If they are males, this leaves them with a hazy and incomplete model for themselves. If they are females, their relations and expectations of men evolve more from fantasy than reality. It seems to me that knowledge about, and familiarity with, the other sex in the growing-up years is a large factor in satisfaction in married life. Furthermore, male absence overdraws on the woman's resources, paving the way for all kinds of destructive results for herself, her children, and her husband. However we slice it, we come into the world with life equipment, but it remains for our experiences to teach the uses of it. After all, the husbands and fathers, the wives and mothers of today are the boys and girls of yesterday.

b. Women who are mothers and men who are fathers could have auxiliary help without stigma in their parenting. Parenting for the first five years is a twenty-four-hour-a-day job. This gets pretty confining if there is no relief. Auxiliary help might go a long way toward breaking the possession aspect of parenthood and move it more toward the real responsibility of developing the child's humanity.

c. There would be family financial allowances to people who needed them, not on the basis of being poor and just making survival possible, but because it was needed to facilitate optimum growth.

d. Preparation for parenting would be seen as something to be actively learned instead of assuming that the experience of conception and birth automatically provided all the know-how one needed. Nobody calling himself an engineer would even be considered for an engineering job if all the preparation he had consisted of his wish to be one, and the knowledge he gained by watching his engineer father.

3. *The idea of developing human beings was considered so important and vital that each neighborhood had within walking distance a Family Growth Center which was a center for learning about being human, from birth to death.* These might well replace public welfare offices, among other institutions. In my opinion, this process, learning how to be human, will never end; I believe the human potential is infinite. We have barely scratched the surface.

4. *The literal context surrounding the birth event included full awareness for the woman giving birth, the active witnessing of the birth process by the father of the child, and the rooming-in of all three for at least the first two weeks.* Everyone would get a chance to be in on the getting-acquainted process that necessarily takes place. In a first birth, the female would meet her husband in his father role for the first time; the male would meet his wife in her mother role for the first time; each would meet a slightly new person. Many men and women feel like strangers to each other when they meet as fathers and mothers despite the fact that they have previously been husbands and wives.

The subsequent celebration following the birth could celebrate not only a birth of a new human being, but a birth of new roles for the adults as well. (The way some celebrations have gone would suggest immaculate conception.) Men often feel like useless appendages at this time. No wonder there are fears of replacement on their part. I wonder whether it would be as possible for men who are fathers to leave their families as readily as they now do if they were part of the literal birth proceedings, openly hailed and honored as being and having been essential, as are women. I wonder too, if this were done, whether the birth of a baby would create as much estrangement between husband and wives as it often does.

5. *Child-rearing practices were changed.*

a. The emphasis in child rearing would be on helping the child find out, crystal-clearly, how he looked and sounded, how to tune in on how he felt and thought, how to find out how he experienced others and affected them, instead of only the admonishment to be good and find out how to please others.

b. From the moment of birth he would be treated as a person with the capacity to hear, to see, to feel, to sense, and to think, different from the adult only in body development and, initially, in putting his sensory and thought experiences into words.

c. He would have a predictable place in time and space.

d. He would have real and openly welcomed opportunities to feel his power and his uniqueness, his sexuality and his competence as soon as his resources permitted it.

e. He would be surrounded by people who openly and clearly enjoyed each other and him, who were straight and real with one another and with him, thus giving him a model for his own delight in interacting with people. Thus, the joy in relationships might overcome the grimly responsible outlook "becoming an adult" often has for a child.

f. "Yes" and "no" would be clear, reliable, appropriate, and implemented.

g. Realness would be valued over approval when there had to be a choice.

h. At every point in time, regardless of age or label, he would always be treated as a whole person and never regarded as too young to be a person.

i. Every child's feelings would be regarded with dignity and respect, listened to and understood; those around him would do the same with each other. There would be a basic difference between his awareness and expression of his feelings and thoughts, and the action he took in relation to them.

j. Every child's actions would be considered separately from his expressions, instead of linking expressions of feeling with an automatic specific act. He would be taught that actions had to be subject to time, place, situation, other persons, and purpose, rather than being given a stereotyped "should" that applies universally.

k. Difference from others would be seen clearly as an opportunity for learning, holding an important key to interest in living and real contact with others, instead of being seen primarily as something to be tolerated, or destroyed, or avoided.

l. Every child would have continuing experience that human life is to be revered, his and that of all others.

m. Every child would openly receive continuing knowledge of how he and all his parts work—his body, his mind, and his senses. He would receive encouragement for expressing, clarifying, and experimenting with his thoughts, his feelings, his words, his actions, and his body, in all its parts.

n. He would look forward to each new step in growth as an opportunity for discovery, encompassing pain, pleasure, knowledge, and adventure. Each phase of growth has special learnings that could be particularly planned for; evidence showing that a new growth step had been achieved would be openly and obviously validated, like celebrating with a party the onset of menstruation for girls and maybe a change of voice party for boys at the time of puberty. Further examples would be: parties for the first step, first tooth, first day at school, first over-night visit with non-familial members, first date, first sexual intercourse, and the first obvious and costly mistake. Mistakes are an inevitable part of risk-taking, which is an essential part of growth, and needs to be so understood.

o. He could see males and females as different, yet interesting and essential to each other, free to be separate instead of being implicit enemies or feeding on each other.

p. He could get training in male-female relations, could prepare openly for mating and parenting in turn, which would be explained as desirable, and demonstrated as such.

q. He would be openly let in on the experiences of adults in parenting, maritalling, and selfing.

6. *He could freely experience in an openly welcoming way the emergence of the sexual self.* This would require lifting the cover of secrecy on the genitals and all that it entails.

7. *The goal of being human was being real, loving, intimate, authentic, and alive as well as competent, productive, and responsible.*

We have never had people reared anything like this on a large enough scale to know how this would affect marriage, the family, and, in general, people-to-people relationships. We have never realized what impetus to a really better world and a socially more evolved people might be created for tackling the "insurmountable" problems of suicide, murder, alcoholism, illegitimacy, irresponsibility, incompetence, war, racial and national conflicts. I think this is worth trying.

In our society, marriage is the social and legal context in which new humans originate and are expected to grow into fully developed human beings. The very life of our society depends upon what happens as a result of marriage. Looking at the institution of marriage as it exists today raises real questions about its effectiveness.

The marriage contract in the Western Christian world has no provision for periodic review or socially acceptable means of termination. I would offer that this contract, as it stands, is potentially inhuman and anti-human, and works against the development of love, trust, and connectedness with other human beings. It is made with the apparent assumption that the conditions present at its inception will continue without change for eternity. This asks people to be wiser than they can possibly be. It is made at a time in the lives of the respective parties when they have the least preparation in fact with which to make this contract.

The contract exacts an explicit agreement that other intimate relationships with the same and the other sex shall cease and each partner shall be the sole resource of total comfort and gratification for the other. Implicitly, the current marriage contract abolishes individual autonomy and makes togetherness mandatory. Independent wishes and acts, or contradictory opinions are seen as threats to marriage

If marriage partners hold on to their integrity and their individuality, their independent wishes and acts, or contradictory opinions, they may retain their integrity but lose the relationship. So, to preserve the marriage, one has to lose one's integrity if to manifest the integrity loses the marriage.

Almost any recent study of the sexual practices of married people reports that many marital partners do not live completely monogamously. Marital partners report from few to many extra-marital sexual relationships, which are largely secret. Frequently-married persons practice a consecutive spousing which is a sort of polygamy done in parts. Mate-swapping, which is polygamy in the open, is becoming more frequent. The myth is monogamy; the fact is frequently polygamy. Evidently, the expectation that each mate should completely suffice the other is failing, and may, by its failure, demonstrate the unreality of this expectation.

Maybe with these facts we have to consider the possibility that human beings are not naturally monogamous.

Maybe monogamy is the most efficient and economic way to organize heterosexual relationships to permit child raising. If so, could monogamy as well as being efficient and economic also be creative, enjoyable, and growth-producing? Maybe this hinges on making possible individual autonomy as well as togetherness. Right now it looks all too often as though monogamy is experienced, after a relatively short time, as grim, lifeless, boring, depressing, disillusioning—a potential context for murder, suicide, mental human decay. Perhaps persons who had rearing of the kind I described would make marriage an exciting and alive experience, and then maybe monogamy could become the rich and fulfilling experience the poets describe.

The marriage contract with its implicit social expectation of chastity is based on the assumption that the expectation of an experience is the same as the actual experience. Chastity all too often disguises ignorance, naivete, and inhibition. These attitudes in too many cases contaminate the marital relationship rather than enhance it.

At this point, I can only fantasy how the sexual relationship in marriage would be changed if the marital partners had been brought up with openness, frankness, love, acceptance, and knowledge of their whole body and that of the other sex.

The current Western marriage contract has been derived from a chattel economic base, which stresses possessing. This frequently gets translated into duty and becomes emotional and sometimes literal blackmail. The quality of joy is lost in the game of scoreboard. "Who loses, who wins, and who is on top?" The result is the grimness I referred to earlier.

Obviously, only mature people can make workable contracts with some hope of achievement, not because they can predict the events, but because they have a workable, growth-producing, coping process to meet whatever comes along. Few people have had open access to the information and experience that could prepare them for being persons, let alone marriage partners.

From the time of puberty the underlying message is be careful of the other sex—the other sex is dangerous. The symbol of this is genital contact, namely intercourse. Many marriages are made by persons who secretly fear that the other sex is dangerous. Out of this is supposed to come intimacy, tenderness, and joining of efforts. How do potential enemies easily translate their relationship into one of intimacy and tenderness?

Maybe there needs to be something like an apprentice period which is socially approved, that precedes an actual marriage, in which potential partners have a chance to explore deeply and experiment with their relationship. This is not exactly a new idea.

In a period of living together, which was socially approved and considered desirable, each could experience the other and find out whether his fantasy matched the reality. Was it really possible through daily living to have a process enabling each to enhance the growth of the other while at the same time enhancing his own? What is it like to have to undertake joint ventures and being with each other every day? It would seem that in this socially approved context, the changes of greater and continuing realness and authenticity would be increased, and the relationship would deepen since it started on a reality base.

Right now such important learning is denied in an effort to preserve the fiction of chastity. It seems to me that this puts undue weight on something that is peripheral to the big goal—healthy, intimate, human relationships.

We have to have a socially accepted and desirable way to terminate a marriage when it appears that it no longer works. What if it could happen just by mutual consent and the only problem was how to plan for the continuing parenting of the children? I doubt that, between people who were authentic and real, this would be either so destructive or so frequent. Human beings with the best intentions and integrity make errors. There needs to be an honorable way to treat this most important error.

If we could truly see that the act of sexual intercourse has much to do with enriching self-esteem in the partners, and that it can represent the highest and most satisfying form of male-female contact, we would be more discriminating. Further, we could openly teach ways to make this possible. To accomplish this we must lift the cover of secrecy and ignorance. At the present time sexual contact is frequently seen as degrading, a form of war, merchandise, lust, a means of scalp-hunting, or as a scoreboard. In these circumstances, when conception results, the child is potentially doomed to the "psychiatric couch," to prison, to poverty, to premature death, or maybe worse yet, to conformity or boredom. How can one degrade or be destructive toward that which he considers openly, truly beautiful and part of his joy in existence?

If we were all to see the sexual act as the renewal value of the other and the increase of self-esteem in the self, if the decision to procreate was a voluntary, mutually-shared one entered into *after* the intimate, satisfying, renewing experience had been achieved by a male and female pair, what magnitude of revolution might we stimulate in a new model for person-to-person relations?

Anyone who has studied family process at all can see with one eye how (1) the sexual relationship is symbolic of the heterosexual inter-relationship and this carries the significance of the person-to-person relationship, and (2) that the fate of the child hangs on this interrelationship.

Intercourse is a fact, not a symbol. Conception, pregnancy, and birth are also facts, not symbols. The child is a result of these facts, but his maturing is guided by the feelings that surround these facts.

I am implying three changes:

1. That the cover of secrecy be removed from the sexual part of the human being. With this cover off, ignorance can be removed.

2. That there be as much attention, care, and implementation, openly, creatively and confidently given to the care, maintenance, and use of the genitals as there is, for instance, to the teeth.

3. That a couple have a means to know when they have achieved intimacy in their relationship, which is based on their experience with, and awareness of, each other as real persons whom they value, enjoy, and feel connected with.

If we were taught from childhood on that our most important goal as human beings is to be real and in continuing touch with ourselves, this in turn would ensure a real connection with others. Were we taught that creativity, authenticity, health, aliveness, lovingness, and productivity were desirable goals, we would have a much greater sense of when this was achieved, and would also find it much easier to do so.

With the expectation of the age of marriage being around twenty and life expectancy being around seventy, close to fifty years of a person's life can be expected to be lived under the aegis of a marriage contract. If the contract does not permit an alive, dynamic experience with growth possible for both, the result is outrage, submission, destructiveness, withdrawal, premature death, or destructive termination. Maybe this type of marriage contract is impossible. If it is, then perhaps what we need to do is to find a way to conceive and bring up children that does not depend on a permanent relationship between the parents. The act of conception and birth could be entirely separated from the process of raising children. We could have child manufacturers and child raisers. We have much of this now except that it is socially stigmatizing. We work awfully hard to make adoption unsuccessful. "He is not my real child," or "She is not my real mother." Actually most of us know that the significance of the blood tie is mostly in our heads.

Maybe the most important thing is that new humans get born and then they are raised. Who does either or both may not be as important as that it is done and how it is done. Maybe if such a "division of labor" were effected, the energies of all the adults of the world would be more available for work and joy and less tied up with what they "should" be.

Procreation—coming about as it does, with little evidence that it will change much in the near future—guarantees that there will always be males and females around, and that they will be attracted to one another, in or out of marriage. Maybe this could be openly acknowledged and we could find ways to use it for our mutual benefit.

As for me, I think a relationship of trust, worth, and love between people is the highest and most satisfying way of experiencing one's humanity. I think this is where real spirituality takes place. Without it, humans become shrivelled, destructive, and desolate.

Right now, our current forms of human interaction, our fears, our suspicions, and our past are working against us. We have all the resources for the needed change, but we do not yet know how to use them. Our survival as a society may well depend upon finding these uses.

6

Progressive Monogamy: An Alternate Pattern?

The very young in our modern society are preoccupied with dreams of love, courtship, and marriage. The newly-weds are preoccupied with adjusting to the dream marriage and, all too soon, with the question: "Is this all there is to it?" Those who fail to find the promised panacea for all personal and societal ills seek a divorce and quickly try again.

We are playing a gigantic game of marital chairs. One out of four who marries this year will divorce and three out of four of those will remarry within the next three years. This drift toward progressive monogamy is not new despite the fact that divorce was considered un-American and incompatible with the American Dream. Divorce was explained away as the escape for the very poor or the very rich, the rebel or the deviant. What *is* new today is the inescapeable fact that serial marriage is now practised by all social classes, both sexes, and all ages.

Yet, even while marriage patterns have been changing, informed analysis is lacking and the search for emerging patterns is most difficult. Will progressive monogamy become an alternate marriage structure within the familial system? Whatever the answer the future may bring, the need to examine honestly what is happening has become a cultural imperative.

For it is true today as never before, that what happens to the cultural forms in our society lies in our own hands. With our greater awareness of the functioning of society, we now know more about the choices available to the individual. In former times, in a world that seemed unchanging, individual choice and personal responsibility were not so great. Today, science and technology are changing society and every one of its institutions. These changes must be accompanied by an increasingly critical evaluation of the individual's role in helping to shape the new cultural forms that are emerging.

Marriage and family patterns are no exception, for they have not escaped the social consequences of industrialization and urbanization. Like all other institutions, they have changed with the changing times. But marriage remains one of the few institutions in which personal autonomy can function and in which the individual still has a sense of personal choice.

Any shift away from the ideal Victorian family—the large, secure, and happy Victorian family—seems to strike at the very heart of the American Dream. Too often such a shift is attacked with moralistic fervor and decried as a disintegration of the family. But is a shift in marriage patterns really a sign of family disintegration? Or does progressive monogamy reflect the appearance of alternatives as the only escape from cultural disaster?

A healthy society requires a healthy family and the family will remain healthy only as it changes to meet the changing needs of society. The large and happy Victorian family may very well be a myth created in our time. Could it also be possible that the bleak future forecast for our present-day family stems from this myth and, therefore, from a failure to recognize and examine reality?

For what is happening to change marriage patterns has been operative since 1890, during the years for which nation-wide data are available. During this period three trends can be observed: (1) the increasing popularity of marriage; (2) the rising incidence of divorce; and (3) the emergence of multiple marriage.

Of these three trends, divorce is the one most carefully reported, the one most deplored as a tragedy to be wept over, rather than analyzed in terms of its "fit" with new life situations. As William Goode comments, "many pretended analyses begin with the well-known rise in divorce rates, and then use selected anecdotes to describe the unfortunate consequences of divorce." [1] This, in the face of the fact that ever since 1890 (except for brief periods in the early 1930's and late 1940's) the rate of increase in divorce has been consistent. No matter how the rate is computed,[2]—the ratio of divorce to the total population, to

---

[1] William J. Goode, *World Revolution and Family Patterns* (Glencoe, Ill., The Free Press, 1963), p. 82.

[2] *U.S. Bureau of the Census Report.*

different age groups here and in other Western countries, or to marriage rates—it has risen steadily. The number of marriages ending in divorce increased from 1 in 12 in 1895 to 1 in 4 in 1960. In 1961 Stuart Queen [3] predicted that one-third to one-half of all marriages occurring in that year "were doomed to failure."

This increase in divorce rates has been accompanied by a steady increase in the percent of marriage. In 1890, 68 percent of all marriageable women had taken the vow, as compared with 58 percent of the men. In the following fifty-year period to 1940 this number had risen to 74 percent of the women and 67 percent of the men. During the next ten years, 1940–1950, a break-down into age groups pointed up two important facts: first, that we are marrying younger than any former generation, and, second, as Ross noted years ago, we are rapidly becoming the most marrying people the world has ever seen. Landis writes, "contrary to popular opinion on the subject, . . . in 1890 only 18.5% of the youth 15–25 years of age were married; in 1947, approximately 30%—an increase of 64%." [4]

This increase continued in the 1960's. But even in other age groups, from 45–49, for example, the percent of those ever married reached 92.2 for women and 91.5 for men. [5] This indicates another shift, the decrease in the gap between the number of men and women who married when compared with the 1890 figures. Our 1960 marriage rate was the largest in the Western world and clearly indicates a shift to marriage as a common life goal for both sexes. The increase in the last years was slight but there was a continuing upward trend. One analyst has gone so far as to predict that we are well on our way toward the day when 85 percent of all those reaching the age of 65 will have been married at least once. All those physically, mentally, emotionally, and religiously able to marry will be doing so.

The third trend, progressive monogamy, is becoming more popular. This practice of taking more than one partner, even though one at a time, lacks adequate documentation for the years from 1890 to 1940. But the figures available indicate that the chances to remarry have

[3] Stuart A. Queen, Robert W. Habenstein, and John B. Adams, *The Family in Various Cultures* (Philadelphia, Lippincott, 1961).

[4] Paul H. Landis, "Sequential Marriage," in the *Journal of Home Economy*, vol. 42 (October, 1950), p. 626.

[5] William J. Goode, *op. cit.*, p. 61.

improved markedly, particularly for young women. This is understandable, and to be expected, in view of the abnormal conditions produced by war throughout this century with the accompanying post-war marriage booms. But, not only are the chances of remarriage for younger women greater now, but the chances for all divorced persons to remarry are higher than for any other category. Paul Landis has shown that, at the age of 30, remarriage is more frequent among divorced than among widowed persons, and higher than first marriages for singles. At this age, a divorced woman's chances are 94 in 100; for the widowed, only 60 in 100; and for the spinster, 48 in 100.[6]

For the male of the same age, the chances for remarriage are 96 in 100; widowed, 92; and the bachelor's chances of marriage, only 67. Even at the age of 40, the divorced woman has 65 chances in 100, the widowed 29, and the single woman 16 in 100. The proportions of families resulting from second, third, fourth and subsequent marriages, is on the increase.

Within these statistics are a number of tantalizing comparisons. William Goode pointed out in a study on steady dating and imminent remarriage that, in the marriage market, the divorced woman who makes herself attractive to men and dates frequently runs "neck to neck" with the divorced woman who has from one to three children and makes little or no attempt to seek a new marriage partner. Is this analagous to the practice anthropologists find among most simpler societies of choosing females who have proven their fertility? Or, perhaps, is this choice of "mothers" a disguised attempt to re-establish the bonds between mothers and sons, so often abruptly broken during adolescence in American society? Goode suggests that American men don't seem able to make up their minds between sex appeal and motherhood.

Gloomy prognostications of family disorganization and disintegration accompany the rising statistics of divorce and remarriage. Yet divorce is universal and there has never been a society in which it has not served as an alternative solution for the unmanageable problems which may arise when two individuals live closely together. In Western cultures, the significance to the individual and to the community of divorce, and of rapid remarriage after divorce, has yet to be studied objectively. If serial marriages continue to increase, what will this mean for the education of children and for the perpetuation of the family?

---

[6] Paul H. Landis, *op. cit.*, p. 625.

Whatever the answer, modern families are engulfed on urban, industrial, bureaucratic, and impersonal relations, and the family has been forced to assume the additional burden for the emotional fulfillment of each member. In simpler societies and in earlier times, this fulfillment was expressed through many other institutions besides the primary family. For in such societies, men use economic and political institutions for personal satisfaction and fulfillment. Work and play outside the home, pride in the individual products of their labor, and a shared responsibility for the welfare of the whole, gave a sense of personal autonomy. Men were not pervaded by a sense of helplessness due to impersonal decisions which affected them drastically but in which they had no voice.

In modern society the family has become the chief means of taking up the slack. Searching for emotional fulfillment on the job and too often failing to find it even in the community, modern man has made marriage a source of all happiness and a solution and compensation for all emotional deprivation. The criterion of a successful marriage is the personal happiness of husband and wife. Mutual compatibility is made the basis for marriage, and marital bliss becomes dependent upon the emotional sentiments (fluctuating and volatile as they may be) with which the couple regard their relationship. Happiness in marriage is thus predicated upon a personal equation, individual satisfaction. This cultural accent upon happiness in the marriage is of relatively recent origin.[7]

The emphasis upon marriage as the major instrument for meeting all problems has been accompanied by a shift from training children for "future" parenthood to preparing them for being a marriage partner. Most societies, and ethnic groups in the United States emphasize "parenthood." Dominant middle-class Americans, however, have chosen to honor "marriage." Little boys as they grow up are taught, not how to be good fathers, but how to be good husbands. Little girls are learning to be attractive wives with false eyelashes, uplift brassieres, and hair-do styles that are "in." Dating is encouraged in the middle elementary grades, and a leading teenage magazine devotes its largest section to menus, not so much for the future mother as for the wife-to-be, as the surest way to a man's heart and hand.

---

[7] John Sirjamaki, "Culture Configuration in the American Family," in the *American Journal of Sociology* (May, 1948), p. 44.

Marriage has become a "dominating life-goal, for men as well as for women. The single adult life, by contrast, according to this attitude, is empty and barren." [8] This covert and all-pervasive value is reflected in social behavior, as girls marry at earlier ages and the average of child-bearing in 1960 was placed at $26\frac{1}{2}$ for the last child. Formerly, the responsibilities of parenthood were sufficient to keep husband and wife together despite personal problems. Now that the goal of happiness—a happiness achieved most quickly through marriage—has pervaded our national life, high expectations that are not fulfilled in everyday life lead to dissolution of wedded bonds. And the pursuit for happiness begins all over again.

What now needs clarification is the tremendous burden that marriage must now sustain. For, currently, multiple marriage is being practiced, not only by the deviants, but also by solid middle-class persons raised on Calvinistic values. Midge Doctor describes the typical young divorcee:

She is in her late twenties, fairly well-educated, with two small children. She was married to a male counterpart of herself, young, a good husband, whom she describes as a "nice guy." She doesn't even say she doesn't love him; rather, she asks, "Is this all there is ever going to be?" Why, then, two and one-half years later, is she again married? . . . The entire adult world is set up for couples and she needs a steady escort.[9]

As the chances for remarriage have improved, some patterns are emerging. Race, religion, education, and age all affect the statistics. Among Negroes the rate is approximately the same as among whites; among Protestants it is somewhat greater than among Catholics; the college woman remarries more frequently than the high-school graduate. Attitudes of friends and families toward divorce and remarriage are important; legal barriers, relaxing laws and, more frequently, changing judicial opinion, all affect the rates of remarriage.

In a culture that teaches "self-fulfillment," anything that creates dissatisfaction with self goes to the very heart of marriage. Marriage, therefore, is openly offered as the solution to all problems of life in our time and culture. Economics, stressed by most authorities as the chief factor underlying divorce, is too simple an answer. In a society like ours,

---

[8] *Ibid.*, p. 465.

[9] Midge Doctor, "The Young Divorcee," in *Harper's Magazine* (October, 1962).

in which economics is a major and all-powerful institution, it is often made the scapegoat for all problems. One authority suggests that women are divorcing more than men today because they are now able to support themselves. Earlier statistics indicate that when self-support was more difficult, women still divorced more often than men. Although economics undoubtedly plays an important role, the future of marriage is being shaped by cultural values, hidden values that pervasively motivate the behavior of human beings. These values suggest an educated guess: that progressive monogamy may very well prove to be an alternate structure for the familial system. Further, it is safe to predict that the future of marriage will be shaped, not so much by economic and utilitarian stresses, as by a new culture configuration brought about by a total readjustment of our society.

7

Marriage in Two Steps[*]

The June bride evokes memory pictures of her mother and her mother's mother as just such a happy girl, caught between tears and laughter. The newest bridegroom, describing his difficulties, awakens memories of other crises, each story a different one, and yet in its happy outcome the same.

For everyone taking part in a wedding each small event, like the solemn ritual of marriage itself, binds the generations in the shared belief that what has been true and lasting in the past is true and lasting today and will remain so safely across time. On such occasions sentiment and loving hope for the young couple—these two who are entering the most important relationship of their adult lives—join in renewing our faith in traditional forms. This, we believe, is how families begin.

But in the cool light of everyday experience a different picture emerges. As a society we have moved—and are still moving—a long way from the kinds of marriage our forefathers knew and believed in. We still define marriage as essentially an adult relationship. But now, in a period in which full participation in adult life is increasingly delayed, the age of first marriage for boys as well as girls has been declining steadily. And although people can look forward to longer years of vigorous maturity, young couples are entering parenthood not later than in the past, but even earlier.

We still believe that marriage entails financial responsibility. Yet we indulge in endless subterfuge to disguise the economic dependency of the majority of very young marriages. Significantly, we have devised systems of loans and insurance to ease our financial burden of seeing children through years of higher education. However, we have not invented any

---

[*] Reprinted from the *Redbook Magazine* (July, 1966), copyright 1966 by McCall Corporation.

form of insurance to cover the care of children born of student marriages, or born to teenage parents who are struggling to find themselves. If we encourage these young marriages, as in fact we do, then we must think more clearly about the long-term economic problems for which we, as parents, may have to take some responsibility.

We still believe that marriage is the necessary prelude to responsible parenthood even though, in every social class, pregnancy is to an increasing extent preceding marriage. We still strongly believe that children born of a marriage should be wanted. In the past, this meant accepting the birth of children no matter what the number and circumstances; but today, with existing methods of conception control, every child could be a chosen child.

We still believe that the continuity of the family, based on marriage, is fundamental to our way of life and to the well-being of every individual child. Yet there is clear evidence of the fragility of marriage ties, especially among very young couples who become parents before they know each other as husband and wife.

The disparities are plain to see and the outlook is unpromising. We might expect this to force us to recognize how great are the discrepancies between our expectations, based on tradition, and what is happening to young American families. The truth is, we have not really faced up to the many conflicts between belief and experience, precept and practice, in our current, muddled style of marriage. It is not enough to say, "Yes, marriage patterns are changing." What we have not fully realized is that we do not have to stand by helplessly while change sweeps over us, destroying our hopes for a better life for our children.

Instead, we can look steadily at the changes that have brought us where we are.

We can ask, "How can we invest marriage forms with new meaning?"

We can move toward a reconciliation of belief and practice that is consonant with our understanding of good human relationships.

Of course, there is no simple way of defining the changes that have already taken place, but two things are crucial in the contemporary attitude—our attitude toward sex and our attitude toward commitment. Today, I am convinced, most Americans have come to regard sex, like eating and sleeping, as a natural activity. We lean toward the belief that persons who are deprived of sex will be tense and crotchety and perhaps unreliable in their personal relationships. We have come to believe also that asking physically mature young people to postpone sex until their middle twenties is neither fair nor feasible. And as we have learned to deal more evenhandedly with boys and girls, most of us have ceased to believe in any double standard of morality. This is in keeping with our belief that sex, like marriage and parenthood, should involve social equals who are close in age. When the age gap widens—when the man is much older than the woman or the woman older than the man—we disapprove. And although we may not express our doubts, we do not have very high expectations for eventual happiness when two people must bridge wide differences in upbringing. We believe that young people should learn about sex together, as equals. But this means that both are likely to be equally inexperienced. Our emphasis, in the ideal, is on spontaneity. It is this combination of beliefs, together with our continuing certainty that sex is safe only in marriage, that has fostered—that has, in fact, forced—our present acceptance of very young marriage.

But in accepting early marriage as the easiest solution to the problem of providing a sex life for everyone, we confront new difficulties. No matter how many books adolescent boys and girls have read, or how freely they have talked about sex, they actually know very little about it and are very likely to bungle their first serious sex relations. Certainly, this is not new; an unhappy honeymoon all too often has been a haunting prelude to marriage. What is new is that the young husband and wife are as yet inexperienced in living through the initial difficulties that can enter into any important adult relationship of choice. They are, for example, inexperienced in making friends and living through the give-and-take that adult friendships require. Young men today rarely know how to make friends with girls, and girls, looking for mates, are unlikely to be much interested in a man as a friend. Heterosexual friendships therefore are postponed until after marriage, and then entered into only with other married couples. Thus, friendship, which ideally should precede marriage and help the young man and woman better understand the adjustments that any adult relationship requires, now comes too late to help a first marriage.

Inexperience is one hazard. But it becomes especially hazardous because we also believe that no one should be trapped in a final mistake. Individuals as they grow and develop are permitted to change their jobs and occupations, to move from one part of the country to another, to form new associations, and develop new interests that bring them into contact with new people. And as part of our expectation that people change as they grow, most of us have come also to accept the idea of divorce. When a marriage does not work out most of us believe each partner should have another chance to start over again with a different man or a different woman. We believe in commitment, but we do not believe that commitments are irrevocable.

But divorce also is a hazard. It is true that for two adults without children who now find that they cannot carry out a commitment made at an earlier stage of their lives, divorce can be an end and a beginning; but because of the role children play in the present style of marriage, divorce becomes a widespread hazard. For whereas in the past a man, and especially a woman, might marry in order to have children, now having a child validates marriage. Pregnancy often precedes marriage, and even where it does not, the style is to have a child quickly. It is as if having a child sets the seal of permanence on a marriage that is in truth far from permanent, and that, at this stage, is still in the making.

The child thus becomes a symbol. This use of a child is out of keeping with our belief that each person should be valued as an individual for his own sake. And when the marriage breaks down, the child is sacrificed to the changed needs of the man and woman, who are acting not as parents but as husband and wife. The child—a person in his own right, growing toward the future—stands as a symbol of an unreal past.

Perhaps we can catch a glimpse of what we might make of marriage and parenthood if we think in terms of a new pattern that would both give young couples a better chance to come to know each other, and give children a better chance to grow up in an enduring family. Through what steps might this be accomplished?

It should be said at once that changes as important as those involved in creating a new style of marriage can never be brought about through the actions of a few people, or even all the members of a single group. In a democracy as complex as ours, in which one must always take into account a great diversity of religious, regional, class, and national styles, success will depend on contributions made by all kinds of people. Many ideas will arise out of discussions in the press, from the pulpits of many churches, on television, in the agencies of government, in the theater, and in community organizations. Some will come from those whose work brings them face to face with the failures of the present system and who are aware of the urgent need for new forms. Some will be shaped by the actual experiments in which lively, imaginative young people are engaging. And still others will arise out of the puzzlement and questions of the people who listen to the suggestions made by all those who are trying to become articulate about the issues. Out of all these discussions, carried on over a period of time, there will, I hope, evolve the kind of consensus that will provide the basis for a new marriage tradition. We are still a long way from the point at which we can consider the new tradition in such pragmatic terms as its formal social framework—in law and religious practice. No one, it should be clear, can write a prescription or make a blueprint for a whole society.

What I am doing here is advancing some ideas of my own as one contribution to an ongoing discussion. First I shall outline the goals that I personally hope we may reach.

I should like to see us put more emphasis upon the importance of human relationships and less upon sex as a physical need. That is, I would hope that we could encourage a greater willingness to spend time searching for a congenial partner and to enjoy cultivating a deeply personal relationship. Sex would then take its part within a more complex intimacy and would cease to be sought after for itself alone.

I should like to see children assured of a lifelong relationship to both parents. This, of course, can only be attained when parents themselves have such a relationship. I do not mean that parents must stay married. As long as early marriage remains a practice, it must be assumed that some marriages—perhaps many marriages—will break down in the course of a lifetime of growth, mobility, and change. But I should like to see a style of parenthood develop that would survive the breaking of the links of marriage through divorce. This would depend on a mutual recognition that co-parenthood is a permanent relationship. Just as brother and sister are irrevocably related because they share the same parents, so also parents are irrevocably related because they share the same child. At present, divorce severs the link between the adult partners and each, in some fashion, attempts —or sometimes gives up the attempt—to keep a separate contact with the children, as if this were now a wholly individual relationship. This need not be.

Granting the freedom of partners to an uncongenial marriage to seek a different, individual commitment within a new marriage, I would hope that we would hold on to the ideal of a lifetime marriage in maturity. No religious group that cherishes marriage as a sacrament should have to give up the image of a marriage that lasts into old age and into the lives of grandchildren and great-grandchildren as one that is blessed by God. No wholly secularized group should have to be deprived of the sense that an enduring, meaningful relationship is made binding by the acceptance, approval, and support of the entire society as witnesses.

At the same time, I believe, we must give greater reality to our belief that marriage is a matter of individual choice, a choice made by each young man and woman freely, without coercion by parents or others. The present mode of seeking for sex among a wide range of partners casually, and then, inconsistently, of accepting marriage as a form of "choice" arising from necessity, is a deep denial of individuality and individual love. In courtship, intensity of feeling grows as two people move toward each other. In our present system, however, intensity of feeling is replaced by the tensions arising from a series of unknown factors: Will pregnancy occur? Is this the best bargain on the sex market? Even with sexual freedom, will marriage result? Today true courtship, when it happens, comes about in spite of, not because of, the existing styles of dating and marrying.

These goals—individual choice, a growing desire for a lifelong relationship with a chosen partner, and the desire for children with whom and through whom lifelong relationships are maintained— provide a kind of framework for thinking about new forms of marriage. I believe that we need two forms of marriage, one of which can (though it need not) develop into the other, each with its own possibilities and special forms of responsibility.

The first type of marriage may be called an *individual marriage* binding together two individuals only. It has been suggested that it might be called a "student" marriage, as undoubtedly it would occur first and most often among students. But looking ahead, it would be a type of marriage that would also be appropriate for much older men and women, so I shall use the term *individual marriage*. Such a marriage would be a licensed union in which two individuals would be committed to each other as individuals for as long as they wished to remain together, but not as future parents. As the first step in marriage, it would not include having children.

In contrast, the second type of marriage, which I think of as *parental marriage*, would be explicitly directed toward the founding of a family. It would not only be a second type but also a second step or stage, following always on an individual marriage and with its own license and ceremony and kinds of responsibility. This would be a marriage that looked to a lifetime relationship with links, sometimes, to many people.

In an individual marriage, the central obligation of the boy and girl or man and woman to each other would be an ethical, not an economic, one. The husband would not be ultimately responsible for the support of his wife; if the marriage broke up, there would be no alimony or support. The husband would not need to feel demeaned if he was not yet ready, or was not able, to support his wife. By the same token, husband or wife could choose freely to support the other within this partnership.

Individual marriage would give two very young people a chance to know each other with a kind of intimacy that does not usually enter into a brief love affair, and so it would help them to grow into each other's life—and allow them to part without the burden of misunderstood intentions, bitter recriminations, and self-destructive guilt. In the past, long periods of engagement, entered into with parental consent, fulfilled at least in part the requirement of growing intimacy and shared experience. But current attitudes toward sex make any retreat to this kind of relationship impossible. In other societies, where parents chose their children's marriage partners, the very fact of meeting as strangers at the beginning of a lifelong relationship gave each a high sense of expectancy within which shared understanding might grow. But this is impossible for us as an option because of the emphasis on personal choice and the unwillingness to insist on maintaining a commitment that has failed.

Individual marriage in some respects resembles "companionate marriage" as it was first discussed in the 1920's and written about by Judge Ben Lindsey on the basis of his long experience in court with troubled young people. This was a time when very few people were ready as yet to look ahead to the consequences of deep changes in our attitude toward sex and personal choice. Today, I believe, we are far better able to place young marriage within the context of a whole lifetime.

Individual marriage, as I see it, would be a serious commitment, entered into in public, validated and protected by law and, for some, by religion, in which each partner would have a deep and continuing concern for the happiness and well-being of the other. For those who found happiness it could open the way to a more complexly designed future.

Every parental marriage, whether children were born into it or adopted, would necessarily have as background a good individual marriage. The fact of a previous marriage, individual or parental, would not alter this. Every parental marriage, at no matter what stage in life, would have to be preceded by an individual marriage. In contrast to individual marriage, parental marriage would be hard to contract. Each partner would know the other well, eliminating the shattering surprise of discovery that either one had suffered years of mental or physical illness, had been convicted of a serious crime, was unable to hold a job, had entered the country illegally, already had children or other dependents, or any one of the thousand shocks that lie in wait for the person who enters into a hasty marriage with someone he or she knows little about. When communities were smaller, most people were protected against such shocks by the publication of the banns. Today other forms of protection are necessary. The assurance thus given to parents that their son or daughter would not become hopelessly trapped into sharing parenthood with an unsuitable mate also would serve as a protection for the children not yet born.

As a couple prepared to move from an individual to a parental marriage they also would have to demonstrate their economic ability to support a child. Instead of falling back on parents, going deeply into debt, or having to ask the aid of welfare agencies, they would be prepared for the coming of a child. Indeed, both might be asked to demonstrate some capacity to undertake the care of the family in the event one or the other became ill. Today a girl's education, which potentially makes her self-sustaining, is perhaps the best dowry a man can give his son-in-law so he will not fall prey to the gnawing anxiety of how his family would survive his death. During an individual marriage, designed to lead to parental marriage, a girl, no less than a boy, might learn a skill that would make her self-supporting in time of need.

Even more basic to the survival of a marriage, however, is the quality of the marriage itself—its serenity, its emotional strength, its mutuality. Over long years we have acquired a fund of experience about good marriages through the inquiries made by adoption agencies before a child is given permanently to adoptive parents. Now, if we wished to do so, we could extrapolate from this experience for the benefit of partners in individual marriages but not yet joined in parenthood and for the benefit of infants hoped for but not yet conceived. And in the course of these explorations before parental marriage the ethical and religious issues that sometimes are glossed over earlier could be discussed and, in a good relationship, resolved. Careful medical examinations would bring to light present or potential troubles, and beyond this, would help the couple to face the issue: What if, in spite of our desire for a family, having a child entails a serious risk to the mother, or perhaps the child? What if, in spite of a good prognosis, we, as a couple, cannot have a child? And then, even assuming that all such questions have been favorably resolved, it must not be forgotten that in all human relationships there are imponderables—and the marriage will be tested by them.

As a parental marriage would take much longer to contract and would be based on a larger set of responsibilities, so also its disruption would be carried out much more slowly. A divorce would be arranged in a way that would protect not only the two adults but also the children for whose sake the marriage was undertaken. The family, as against the marriage, would have to be assured a kind of continuity in which neither parent was turned into an angry ghost and no one could become an emotional blackmailer or be the victim of emotional blackmail.

Perhaps some men and women would choose to remain within individual marriage, with its more limited responsibilities; having found that there was an impediment to parental marriage, they might well be drawn into a deeper individual relationship with each other. And perhaps some who found meaningful companionship through parenthood would look later for more individualized companionship in a different kind of person.

By dignifying individual relationships for young people we would simultaneously invest with new dignity a multitude of deeply meaningful relationships of choice throughout life. First and foremost, we would recognize parenthood as a special form of marriage. But we would also give strong support to marriage as a working relationship of husband and wife as colleagues, and as a leisure relationship of a couple who have not yet entered into or who are now moving out of the arduous years of multiple responsibilities.

By strengthening parenthood as a lasting relationship we would keep intact the link between grandparents, parents, and children.

Whether they were living together or were long since divorced, they would remain united in their active concern for their family of descendants. The acceptance of the two kinds of marriage would give equal support, however, to the couple who, having forgone a life with children, cherish their individual marriage as the expression of their love and loyalty.

The suggestion for a style of marriage in two steps—individual marriage and marriage for parenthood—has grown out of my belief that clarification is the beginning of constructive change. Just as no one can make a blueprint of the future, so no one can predict the outcome of a new set of principles. We do know something about the unfortunate direction in which contemporary marriage is drifting. But we need not simply continue to drift. With our present knowledge, every child born can be a child wanted and prepared for. And by combining the best of our traditions and our best appraisal of human relations, we may succeed in opening the way for new forms of marriage that will give dignity and grace to all men and women.

8

Group Marriage:
A Possible Alternative?

One of the types of marriage that seems to have always existed during the history of humanity is group marriage. In its strictest form it consists of a relatively small number of adults—say, from four to fifteen—living together, sharing labor, goods, and services, bearing and raising their children in common, and engaging in promiscuous sex relations, so that every male in the group has intercourse, at one time or another, with every female in the group. In its looser form, it consists of communal or tribal marriage, where a larger group of adults—say, up to several hundred individuals—live in a single co-operative community and have at least theoretical sexual access to all other members of the same community, although actually, in a year's time, a particular member of this sexual-economic cooperative may engage in intercourse and potentially procreate with only a few other members of the large group.

Small-scale group marriage has apparently been reasonably common throughout human history, and definitely exists in various parts of the United States and the rest of the world today. Group marriages of this kind do not usually remain viable for any considerable period of time, but keep breaking up for one reason or another—with some of the members, who are quite devoted to this kind of living, thereafter seeking and founding another small-scale group marriage arrangement in a different house or another community.

Large-scale or tribal forms of group marriage that have existed for even a few months at a time seem to have been rare in human annals. Many mythical ones have been reported over the years, but authentic instances—such as that of the perfectionist Oneida Community in upstate New York which lasted for thirty years during the middle of the nineteenth century[1]—have seldom been shown to exist.

The anthropological and sociological literature of the late nineteenth century was occupied—indeed, almost obsessed—with the question of whether primitive man generally lived in a state of group marriage. As Westermarck notes:

It is often said that the human race must have originally lived in a state of promiscuity, where individual marriage did not exist, where all the men in a horde or tribe had indiscriminate access to all the women, and where the children born of these unions belonged to the community at large. This opinion has been expressed by Bachofen, McLennan, Morgan, Lord Avebury, Giraud-Teulon, Lippert, Kohler, Post, Wilken, Kropotkin, Wilutzky, Bloch, and many others.[2]

Among those cited by Westermarck, we may quote Lord Avebury who strongly stated that

My position was that no such institution [as marriage] existed amongst our primitive ancestors, and that they lived in a state of what, for want of a better term, I propose to call "communal marriage." This has been admitted by some high authorities, but questioned by others, who do not seem, however, to be always consistent, and while denying it in some passages, appear to admit it in others.[3]

Iwan Bloch was, if anything, even stronger in his belief that monogamous or even polygamous marriage, as we know these forms of family relationships, did not exist among early man:

Whoever knows the nature of the sexual impulse, whoever has arrived at a clear understanding regarding the cares of human evolution, and finally, whoever has studied the conditions that even now prevail among primitive peoples and among modern civilized races in the matter of sexual relations,

---

[1] John H. Noyes, *History of American Socialism* (Philadelphia, Lippincott, 1870).

[2] Edward Westermarck, *The History of Human Marriage* (New York, Macmillan, 1925), vol. 1, p. 103

[3] Lord Avebury, *The Origin of Civilization and the Primitive Condition of Man* (London, Longmans, Green, 1912 ed.), p. 3.

can have no doubt whatever that in the beginnings of human development a state of sexual promiscuity did actually prevail.[4]

Sir James G. Frazer, another great authority on primitive peoples, also strongly believed in the prevalence of group marriage in early times:

Exogamy . . . has everywhere been originally a system of group marriage devised for the sake of superseding a previous state of sexual promiscuity. . . . It appears to be a reasonable hypothesis that at least a large part of mankind has passed through the stage of group-marriage in its progress upward from a still lower stage of sexual promiscuity. . . . The age of sexual promiscuity belongs to a more or less distant past, but clear traces of it survive in the right of intercourse which in many Australian tribes the men exercise over unmarried girls before these are handed over to their husbands. . . . Even these customs are by no means cases of absolutely unrestricted promiscuity, but taken together with the converging evidence of the series of exogamous classes they point decidedly to the former prevalence of far looser relations between the sexes than are now to be found among any of the Australian aborigines.[5]

On the other hand, many authorities have violently disputed the notion that group marriage was a general pattern early in human history. Arthur James Todd notes that

On the whole, the evidence is inconclusive for the former universality of group-marriage. I do not consider it necessary to assume that the race passed through this stage in the evolution of familial forms. Our own conclusion is that group-marriage has not yet been sufficiently established to build extensively upon. . . . We should be prepared to find in primitive society a varying condition of promiscuity and fixity in the marriage relation, which we might briefly term intermittent promiscuity.[6]

William Graham Sumner opposed the theory of primitive promiscuity since he felt that any kind of marriage worthy of the name means regulation, and regulation and pure promiscuity are incompatible:

[4] Iwan Bloch, *The Sexual Life of Our Time* (New York and London, Rebman, 1908), p. 188.

[5] James G. Frazer, *Totemism and Exogamy* (London, Macmillan, 1910), vol. IV, pp. 110–111, 137, 151.

[6] Arthur James Todd, *The Primitive Family* (New York, Putnam, 1913), pp. 31–44.

The existence of the marriage institution means restriction upon the sex relation. If there ever was a time of no restriction, that was a time when marriage was absent. Since available evidence leads to the conclusion that there was less of regulation upon the earlier stages of institutional evolution than later, it is a logical inference that the slight restriction encountered under the most primitive of conditions was preceded by no regulation at all—none, that is to say, in the *mores*. . . . Evidence of this order is conclusive for a very slight degree of regulation, if not of utter promiscuity; however, cases of no regulation at all, that is, of the utter absence of marriage, are about as rare in ethnography as those of no religion. . . . What men did before the formation of society is a matter of considerable indifference to us, but we cannot see that any human society could have established itself or could have long endured without subjecting the sex relation to control. We prefer, therefore, to speak of minimal regulation or relative unregulation rather than of promiscuity.[7]

The hypothesis that early man regularly and universally practiced tribal promiscuity or large-scale group marriage was thoroughly investigated and dealt what has been accepted as practically a death blow by Edward Westermarck, who concluded in this connection:

It is not, of course, impossible that among some peoples the intercourse between the sexes may have been almost promiscuous. But the hypothesis according to which promiscuity has formed a general stage in the social history of mankind . . . is in my opinion one of the most unscientific ever set forth within the whole domain of sociological speculation.[8]

As far as I can see, Westermarck was most probably right in this conclusion. It should be noted, however, that he merely stated that tribal promiscuity never seems to have been a *general* custom among primitive peoples. He does not say that it never existed at all, and he by no means rules out the occurrence, many times during history, of separate instances of small-scale group marriage. As Baber notes:

The human family has not universally gone through a uniform series of stages in its evolution—there is every reason to believe that the development of the

---

[7] William Graham Sumner and Albert G. Keller, *Science of Society* (New Haven, Yale University Press, 1927), pp. 1547–1549.

[8] Edward Westermarck, *op. cit.*, vol. 1, p. 336.

family was sometimes random and sometimes opportunistic, as has been the case in the evolution of many other phases of culture.[9]

So, in all probability, group marriage has been with us from primitive times onward. Modern manifestations of this form of sex-love relationship are definite but hardly startling. Because I am one of the recognized leaders in the field of sexual liberalism, and have written a good many articles and books espousing premarital sex relations and free love unions,[10] many individuals and groups in the United States have been in touch with me during the past decade and have told me of their sex doings and problems. As a result of written and personal contact with these people, I have been apprized of the existence, from time to time, of about a dozen group marriage arrangements. Usually, these have been established by utopian-minded individuals who band together, in groups of from four to ten adults, live under one roof (generally in some western or midwestern part of the country), work cooperatively together, and engage in round-robin type of sex relationships. That is to say, few sexual orgies of any kind take place, but the males and females in the group keep pairing off, from day to day, with different partners, so that each group member regularly copulates with all the other members of the opposite sex.

As far as I can tell from communications from my correspondents, these group marriages last from about several months to a few years, and then seem to break up for one reason or another, particularly for nonsexual reasons. Thus, some of the members of the cooperative will not work steadily at the jobs they are supposed to perform, or they will exhibit personality traits that are highly distasteful to some of the other group members. Hence a breakup will occur.

In addition to my personal knowledge of American group marriages, there are reliable literature reports of a good many such arrangements during the last decade:

1. The Kerista movement was started several years ago and reports

---

[9] Ray E. Baber, *Marriage and the Family* (New York, McGraw-Hill, 1939), p. 59.
[10] Albert Ellis, *The Case for Sexual Liberty* (Tucson, Seymour Press, 1965); *idem, Sex Without Guilt* (New York, Lyle Stuart and Grove Press, 1965); *idem, The Search for Sexual Enjoyment* (New York, Macfadden-Bartell, 1966); *idem, If This be Sexual Heresy . . .* (New York, Lyle Stuart and Tower Publications, 1966); *idem, Sex and the Single Man* (New York, Lyle Stuart and Dell Books, 1966).

on its activities have regularly appeared in its newspaper, *The Kerista Tribe*, in *The Modern Utopian*, and in various other publications. For a while its leaders, Jud Presmont and Dau, tried to get an active group started on Roatan Island, British Honduras, but were harassed by immigration regulations and lack of proper medical facilities; "the number of people who said they were coming down was many and the number of people who came down with the right spirit and attitude was few."[11] Kerista is very openly devoted to group sex-love relations, and has had active communities going, at various times, in New York City, Los Angeles, San Francisco, and elsewhere.

The history of Kerista has been one of continual trouble, with new members coming into the fold, staying for a while, and then leaving. As Presmont notes:

One of the biggest problems in the utopian communal thing is strangers—constant strangers—most of whom are dilettantes and dabblers, who come into your life in a steady flow and haven't the slightest interest in what's happening except perhaps to meet a new girl or a new man who'll make a marriage prospect and who can be pulled out of the communal thing into the other society. Anyway, we're learning more about it every day.[12]

2. The hippie movement began a few years ago, largely in the Haight-Ashbury section of San Francisco, and then spread in a big way to New York City's lower East side. The hippies are largely interested in "turning on" to psychedelic experiences, especially through taking marijuana and LSD; in dropping out of the Establishment and living in unconventional ways; and in love and community spirit, at least as far as their fellow members are concerned.[13] One of the common hippie customs is to have several males and females share an apartment (or "pad"), undress and sleep in the same room (with eight or ten of them often sleeping on mattresses or other make-shift beds at the same time), and have group sex relations. Although

[11] Jud Presmont, "Kerista Tribe," in *Modern Utopian*, vol. 1, no. 5 (1967), pp. 11–12.

[12] *Ibid.*, p. 12.

[13] Julio Mitchel, "Galahad's Pad," in *Avant Garde*, vol. 1, no. 1 (January, 1968), pp. 10–15; Earl Shorris, "Love is Dead," in *New York Times Magazine* (October 29, 1967), pp. 113–116; and "The Hippies," *Time Magazine* (New York, Time-Life Books, 1967).

the hippies who share the same bedroom may not stay together for very long (some for a day, some for weeks or months), there is no question that at times they maintain a form of group marriage, and that all the females in the group sexually share the same males, and *vice versa*.

Communal marriage among the hippies, however, usually is quite limited. As Shorris notes:

Sex in the hippie world belongs to the seniors; the freshmen just arrived from Connecticut and Minnesota find there are five boys to every girl and the girls want the drug peddlers or musicians or any boy who has established himself as the hippie version of the letter man. The best the freshman can hope for is occasional group sex in a crash pad, a homosexual experience, or a gang rape.[14]

Paul Krassner also wonders whether the hippies are truly and liberally devoted to group sex as, on the surface, they sometimes seem to be:

It's possible that many hippies indulge in mysticism because they have enough of a puritan hangover that they can't accept pleasure on its own terms; they have to rationalize it with spirituality.[15]

3. Various other reports of group marriage appear from time to time in the literature on the Sexual Freedom League, the Rene Guyon Society, the Sexual Emancipation Movement, and various other sexually liberal organizations. Thus, H. Wayne Gourley reports that "The Amity Community, which existed from 1959 to 1963, practiced it with impressive results. Little experimentation has been done to determine how much group marriage is optimal. The widest example of group marriage practiced today is found among the mate-swappers. Of course, this is a partial group marriage, but is quite successful." [16]

From all these reports, it can be seen that group marriage unquestionably exists today in the United States and in other parts of

---

[14] Earl Shorris, *op. cit.*, p. 113.

[15] Paul Krassner, "Blow-up: Psychedelic Sexualis and the War Game," in *Realist*, vol. 1, no. 75 (June, 1967), p. 19.

[16] H. Wayne Gourley, "A Utopian Answer: Walden House *Plus* Group Marriage," in *Modern Utopian*, vol. 1, no. 1 (1967), p. 36.

the world. But it leads a somewhat checkered career, never seems to become exceptionally well-established, and is largely practiced by unstable groups which have a hard time getting started and an even more difficult time remaining in existence.

Is, then, group marriage a possible alternative for the conventional kind of monogamous—or, rather, monogynous—marital relationship that now normally exists in Western civilization? Not in the strict sense of the term: if alternative is taken to mean a choice between two things. For it is highly unlikely that group marriage will ever fully replace monogamic mating, or even that the majority of Westerners will voluntarily choose it instead of our present marital system.

This is not to say that monogamy does not have its distinct disadvantages, for, of course, it does. It leads to monotony, to restrictiveness, to possessiveness, to sexual starvation for many unmarried individuals, to the demise of romantic love, and to many other evils.[17] Consequently, it has always tended to be seriously modified by virtually all peoples who have legally adopted it. Thus, in present-day America, we ostensibly marry only one member of the other sex and stay married to him or her for the remainder of our lives. Actually, however, we have very frequent resort to divorce, adultery, premarital sex relations, prostitution, promiscuous petting outside of marriage, and various other forms of non-monogamous sex relations. So our "monogamy" is honored more often in theory than in practice.

Group marriage, however, at least when it is practiced by a relatively small number of people, involves many serious difficulties and disadvantages, and is therefore not likely to become exceptionally popular. Among its distinct shortcomings are these:

1. It is quite difficult to find a group of four or more adults of both sexes who can truly live harmoniously with each other. The usual kind of utopian-minded individual who seeks out such group marriages today is very frequently a highly peculiar, often emotionally disturbed, and exceptionally freedom-loving individual. But group marriage in many ways is not suited to this type of person, because it involves restrictions, restraints, and the kind of self-discipline that he has great trouble in achieving.

[17] Albert Ellis, *The American Sexual Tragedy* (New York, Lyle Stuart and Grove Press, 1962); *idem, The Case for Sexual Liberty* (Tucson, Seymour Press, 1965).

2. Even perfectly well-adjusted individuals in our society seem to have difficulty living together successfully in the same household with several other people. Cooperative living of this sort usually involves the scheduling of shopping, cleaning, eating, television-viewing, music-listening, and many other activities at certain times and places which are not going to be particularly convenient to several members of the community-living group. It is often hard enough for two people who love each other to stay together for long periods of time under the same roof, considering that they both are different persons and have all kinds of domestic and other tastes and interests; consequently, many otherwise fairly good monogamic marriages founder. When from four to fifteen people, with even more varying preferences and goals, try to live together continually, many toes are bound to get trod upon and the fur is often likely to fly.

3. Selecting a suitable group of several other individuals with whom one would like to have a group marriage arrangement often proves to be well nigh impossible. It should be remembered, in this connection, that many bright and charming people find it most trouble-some to find even a single member of the other sex whom they can fully trust and with whom they would like to settle down to domestic bliss. When these same people go out to search for several others to "marry" simultaneously, and when they also have to find others who are compatible themselves, it can readily be seen that an enormous selectivity problem arises. Even a highly efficient computer which is fed suitable data on tens of thousands of individuals, and thereby is able to "know" their own characteristics and their likes and dislikes regarding others, will be hard put to select marital groups of, say, four males and four females who can beautifully tolerate—not to mention, love!—each other for a considerable period of time. Simple wife-swapping, as it is sometimes carried on today, where a hetero-sexual couple try to find another heterosexual couple with whom to swap mates, largely for sexual purposes alone, tends to run into selection troubles, simply because if John and Jane find Hal and Helen, who are both sexually attractive to them, they then have to find that Hal and Helen also find *them* attractive and are willing to swap mates. Because of this selectivity problem, many couples who are quite eager to engage in mate-swapping actually rarely get around to doing so. Imagine, then, how hard it would be for John and Jane, if they wanted to join a group marriage household, to find a suitable Hal and Helen,

Matthew and Mary, and Bob and Betty—all of whom would also have to be "sent" by each other!

4. If three or four couples do manage to set up a group marriage arrangement, sex and love problems are almost certain to arise among them. Thus, Jane may get so devoted to Harold that she only wants to be with him or to have sex with him alone. Or Bob may be perfectly potent with Helen and Mary, but not with Jane and Betty. Or Helen may be highly attractive to all the males, while the rest of the girls are not. Or Betty may be the least attractive of the females and may want to have sex relations with the males more than all the other girls do. Or Matthew, who may be the sexiest one of all the males, and the one whose presence really induced most of the females to join the group, may get disenchanted with most of the females and may engage in adulterous affairs outside the group. Or Jane may become so jealous of the other girls, because she thinks they are prettier or more competent than she is, that she may play nasty tricks on them and disrupt the household. All kinds of sex, love, and jealousy problems such as these may easily arise in any sex commune.

5. In our own society, there appear to be fewer females than males at the present time who are interested in group marriage. In Kerista and in hippie groups this phenomenon has often been discovered and has led to the disruption of the groups. Kathleen Griebe [18] reports that in the utopian community that was established at Walden House a few years ago, difficulty arose on the subject of group marriage, which was favored by the founder of the community, H. Wayne Gourley, and consequently Mr. Gourley had to resign from the organization and sold the house to the remaining members.

Miss Griebe notes that

group marriage was not defeated at Walden House by a "vote." The simple fact is that there has never been a female at Walden House who had any interest in group marriage. . . . The day when a group of members within Walden House finds itself personally inclined to experiment with group marriage, they will simply do so, without anybody's permission or vote or consensus. Everybody here minds his own business strictly in these matters. In the meantime the idea suffers, as I said from the lack of a single female interested in making the experiment. [19]

[18] Kathleen Griebe, "Walden House Talks Back," in *Modern Utopian*, vol. 1, no. 2 (1967).   [19] *Ibid.*, p. 2.

Along with these disadvantages of group marriage, there are of course various advantages, including the following:

1. It affords a considerable degree of sexual varietism. If four or more adults get together on a group marriage basis, they all have sexual access to each other; if enough males and females are members of the marital group, two individuals may have intercourse with each other relatively infrequently, even though each of them is having rather frequent sex relations on the whole. This kind of varietism may well serve to keep the participants more sexually alive than they otherwise would be, and to make steady marital relations unusually tolerable.

2. Group marriage widens and enhances love relationships for many individuals. Such people do not merely want to limit themselves to loving one member of the other sex at a given time, but feel that they can intensely love at least several other people. In group marriage, they have the opportunity to relate to, and live with, two or more members of the other sex. Assuming that they can find suitable partners in this respect, they feel much more fulfilled than they otherwise would.

3. Family life can be increased and intensified by group marriage. Instead of merely having one wife and a few children, all of whom may have rather different interests than his own, a man may have several wives and a good many children, some of whom are more likely to share his own vital absorptions. He may also find it more gratifying, for a number of reasons, to share family life with a relatively large, rather than a relatively small, number of people and may discover that his desires for close kinship are only met in this kind of an unusual manner.

4. Group marriages almost always constitute themselves as some kind of a cooperative living arrangement; this has economic and social advantages for many individuals. Thus, a ménage consisting of, say, six adults and ten children can economically share expenses in a large house; can nicely collaborate on shopping, cooking, cleaning, baby-sitting, and other household tasks; can easily arrange for social contacts and outlets; can work together on their own estate; can own expensive equipment, such as a truck or tractor, that smaller families might not be able to afford; can maintain a good measure of economic security even if some of the adult members are temporarily out of work; and can have many other benefits that would not be easily available to a single couple and their children.

5. Group marriage tends to add an experiential quality to human existence that is likely to be absent or reduced in monogamic mating. Under monogamy (or, for that matter, polygyny) a woman tends to marry at an early age and to have long-term relations with one man and a few children for the rest of her life. Her intense and deep encounters with other human beings, therefore, tend to be quite limited; by the time she dies, it is questionable whether she has ever truly lived. If this same woman participates for a number of years in a group marriage, it is almost certain that she will have multifaceted sex, love, child-rearing, and other human relations that she would otherwise never have, and that she may thereby know herself as a person much better and develop along several fulfilling lines that she easily could have failed to know. And the same thing goes, though perhaps to a lesser degree, for the average male in our society, who today only has one or two monogymous marital experiences.

6. Those individuals who are primarily interested in gaining a sense of the brotherhood of man, and in loving and living cooperatively with a fairly large segment of their surrounding population may partially achieve this goal by participating in a group marriage. In this kind of a situation, they can devote themselves to a larger segment of humanity, in a highly personalized way, than they ordinarily would be able to do, and may find this quite satisfying.

For reasons such as these, it is likely that some individuals will always favor some kind of group marriage, especially in theory, and that some will even find it good in actuality. There seems to be no reason why such people should not be enabled to practice what they preach, since there is no evidence that they will thereby interfere with the rights of others, who want to engage in monogamic, polygamic, or various other types of marriage.

It seems very doubtful, however, that a great many people will rush into group marriages in the near future; it seems even more unlikely that this form of mating and family life will replace monogamy or polygamy on a world-wide or even a national scale. Group sexuality —where three or more adults get together in the same room or in different rooms for the purposes of mate-swapping, heterosexual orgies, bisexual orgies, and other forms of plurisexual combinations— has already increased significantly in the United States during the last decade, and is likely to increase more, as men and women become liberated from puritanical notions of what sex should be. It is even possible that within the next fifty years or so most Americans will participate, at some time or other, in some kind of simultaneous sex relationships. But it is highly probable that they will do so on an intermittent or temporary basis, rather than steadily, in the course of a group marriage arrangement.

Group marriage, then, is a logical alternative to monogamic and to other forms of marriage for a select few. In practice, marriage tends to be monogynous (that is, a man and a woman living fairly permanently, though not necessarily forever, only with each other and their own children) all over the world, even when other forms of mating are legally allowed. The chances are that this kind of practice will largely continue, but that a sizeable minority of individuals will devise interesting variations on this major theme or else live in thoroughly non-monogamic unions, including group marriage.

9
Polyandry and Polygyny: Viable Today?

Jim

Jim had closed the door and was leaving Ann behind in her house. They had talked and walked, gone to the movies and to bed, cleaned up the house and various bills, listened to music and themselves, and now he was leaving and was going into a new world in which Ann had no place for the time being. As good a time as they had had, he was now free of her and her ways. But it had been nice—notwithstanding the blowup Tuesday night over the bills—it had been nice. To Ann he could always be strong and let her rest and cuddle against him. And she had learned not to ask questions. Must be tough on her, but that's the way it is. And now he had closed the door.

Victoria, of course, expected him. In fact, she was out in the yard. The mail had just come and she waved at him with letters in her hand as he came out of the car. They hugged and she rubbed her hands over his arms and shoulders, and it felt to him as if she were working her fingers into the material, almost into the material of him, so strong was the impact. They went inside. The wonder of her, the way she looked at you. He felt that she read his mind the way she looked at him. She said, "You think we should talk first or get into bed first?" "Right," he said. "When I come to you I am always torn. I don't want to treat you just as a thing, but God, I'm turned on so. So strongly it's hard to keep my hands off you." He went over and while she muttered—"But you know I feel the same," they fell over each other. No, they never made it to the bed. He came on so strongly that it was over with before it had a chance to be consummated. He was so chagrined, but she only laughed and that helped. "Later," she said as she scrambled up. He came back out of the bathroom and she had prepared some food, sardines on toast. "Oh, she knows me well," he thought. "She, Vicky." And Ann flashed into his mind. "What is Ann doing now? On the phone for her boss no doubt." And then he obliterated Ann. Ann disappeared into a telephone wire on the horizon, then into a fluffy cloud that curled into the sky . . . away . . . gone.

The smell of sardines was overpowering. "I've been thinking," said Vicky, "that Norwegians have been exporting sardines for years. Are they in the Common Market?" The talk drifted to economics, the damage of a windstorm to the house, the population problem in India, and before long their feelings of affection had overpowered them again. Though this time they paced the tempo of their engines and it all came off well. "Was this love?" he thought. That word brought Ann back in and he knew then that he had said sentences with love in it to Ann not too long ago. Vicky had her back to him and as he contemplated that picture of her back he repeated to himself, "Love, love, love—but I feel what I feel and this is what I feel . . ." "Jim," Vicky brought him back. "Rub my back." And so he rubbed her back. She purred, a good sound making gooseflesh. Geese flying. He wrote big letters into the sky . . . V-I-C-T-O-R-I-A. "Jim," she said. "Jim."

They slept—they shopped, they ate dinner, they went to a concert, they went to bed, they made love again, and they slept.

Then it was Monday and he went off to the office. He called her at noon—the first day after he was back with Vicky he had trouble dialing her number—Ann's was too fresh in his mind—but Vicky's voice clear and direct said, "James, you'll be here tonight, do you know what that means?" "Yes, it means you are cooking dinner for two," he said. "Right," she said, "for two. I won't have to be alone. Do you know how lonely it is during the stretch when you are not here?" (How they avoided saying openly, "when you are with her." When they had done that in the beginning it had spoiled things so.) "Do you realize what it is to be by oneself? Of course, you don't," she said. "She probably wants to call me a bastard," he thought, "but she doesn't." "Vicky," he said, "no, I probably don't really know. Look now, don't let it get you down now. Five hours and I'll be there."

He brought her a candy bar, a ten cent bar, a Hershey. She tore the wrapper off impatiently—there it was again—Ann would have probably taken the candy out of the paper and thrown the wrapper into the wastepaper basket, offered him a bite and then taken one herself. All of a sudden he disliked Vicky, her directness and coarseness. She must have noticed something because she poked him and said, "Don't you like your little piggy?" He almost slapped her in the face then, but caught himself and patted her on the bottom instead, converting the anger into contact with her femaleness and it brought him back to reality. A reality that contained Vicky and him in this cozy kitchen with Monk playing a hard piano on the phonograph; liver, which he loved, smelling up the air; and Vicky after all saying to him, "Go, goose, read the mail. Dinner will be ready in fifteen minutes."

He went up to the john and there was a note pinned to his towel. The note read, "Towels are like skin—you remember?" Yes, he remembered how he had toweled her off after their first shower together and how she had revelled in the touch of the towel stroking her bottom and daring it for the first time—his cheek rubbing the same spot and her even greater delight at that. Towels. And then he saw rushing out of the darkness of his imagination Ann's bathroom. The dainty curtains and pink washcloths. He shook his head as if to brush that picture aside, but Ann seemed to come right out of her shower toward him and he hurriedly left the bathroom sniffing the air to be reminded of Vicky. And there she was in slacks and sweater, cigarette in her mouth, and a glass of sherry in her hand, looking at *Newsweek* magazine. She glanced at the kitchen timer, "Baked potatoes will be done in seven minutes. Give me a bit more sherry. Did you know Bernstein's retiring from the New York Philharmonic? He wants to compose full time. You like Jews?" And then they laughed over the old "Some of my best friends are. . . ." It never made any difference. It could have. They had talked that out at the time. The residue of some of those feelings. I suppose one never gets completely over them. It was good that Ann liked Jews. There it was again, Ann. Ann Lillegren, blonde and Scandinavian. Go away Ann, go away. He looked at Vicky and she blew smoke in his face. (She must know sometimes what was going on in his mind.) His concern must have shown. Vicky said, "Don't fret so, let's eat."

She brought up the point of loneliness after dinner. He had his head on her lap—they were on the couch. "When you called me and we talked about how hard these times without you are I didn't want to bug you, and really, I survive quite well, but you really ought to know what this place is like without you. A bore, really, and I get tempted to try the system for me, too. Why shouldn't I? I don't want to, that's why. Maybe in the future but not now. I suppose I could love others, but at this time in my life I really want no one else. How does Ann feel?"

The surprise of Ann's name hanging there in the air was complete. He sat up and wanted to say, "You shouldn't have." The unbroken rule had been broken, but all he managed to say was, "Ann does have another. She can't stand to be alone."

So that was that. Silence now. Vicky and Jim both retreating from this delicate territory back to safety. His head back in her lap and she sliding her hand over his face and hair—the liver smell was too penetrating and they opened the windows widely. "Let's take a walk." "Yes, let's. It might rain so let's take raincoats." "Better close the windows." "Yes." They went for a walk.

Before going to sleep that night and Vicky asleep already, Jim was thinking, "So different they are—the way I wanted it—Ann, I think of her here—almost like something seeping in from the outside. Funny, seeping in, what a word, never gets in though, really. Vicky is there, all the way there, such a lot of Vicky. Vicky. Victoria." He turned to her and curled around her and fell asleep.

Fran

The car disappeared out of the driveway and Fran followed it all the way. "I have to go shopping," she thought. "I am out of practically everything. I better wait for Greg though. He likes to go to the market and tell me what to get. I am in for soups. God that man loves soups day and night. I wonder if he likes mock turtle, yeah, he eats soups day and night. Night. I better do a bit of cleaning too. Phil sure doesn't care. Phil, good boy. Phil gone away for a month now. Go away from my window Phil," she hummed, "go away from my door."

She went upstairs and scrubbed the bathroom tiles, threw linen and towels in the hamper and brought out fresh things and folded the towels neatly. "That's Greg for you," she thought, "everything has to be in place. Crazy. Maybe Phil is too much of a slob, but what a comfortable good-natured slob." Her musing was interrupted by a bang on the door and then a loud voice. "Where are you honey?" And there was Greg, 6' 2", a big brute and she ran downstairs and into his bearhug. Greg had come in with two huge suitcases which were now standing in the middle of the hall. He viewed them, then swiftly took one in each hand and carried them upstairs to get them out of the way. Fran had cleared plenty of drawers for him and space in the closet. She knew he would be restless until he had put things away and changed from his business suit into khakies and polo shirt. So she went upstairs with him because she knew that's the way he wanted it. "Run me a tub sweetie," he said and she knew what that meant too. "Sorry bud, you gotta wait another day Greg." "Oh, no." "Oh, yes," she said. He grabbed her and she wanted him too, but he would have to wait until the next day. So he took a tub and came down spic and span. "A well scrubbed guy," Fran thought. "It's nice to be seen with him. I like to be in his company, with people wondering about us." And she wouldn't have to back the car out of the garage. Damn that driveway anyway. But Greg would handle that car like a toy. That big man had such a gentle touch. He slapped her on the rump. "Fran," he said, "I brought you something." With that he came up with a package from behind his back. Inwardly Fran groaned, "The usual ten pair of hose." To her surprise, however, he had taken the last discussion about gifts to heart and she unwrapped a pair of very pretty earrings. She was stunned if not shocked, but almost immediately panicked as her hands went to her ears. Had she taken Phil's earrings off? Yes, by God, she had. Greg looked at her as her hands were dropping down again. Had he guessed? Perhaps he had. Why shouldn't he? After all, reality. She remembered when she and Phil had gone to that party and this social psychologist had talked about gregariousness. The word had made her look up only to see Phil smile at her. He knew and he understood.

"Greg, you didn't. . . ." How corny that sounded, "You did." So that was good and he had also remembered to pay the insurance premium and he had brought a picture album to put her photos in, and he inquired about her kidneys and wondered if she still had to go so much. "Don't worry, silly. I'm OK. I really am. Let's go out and get some groceries." "You waited. Hmmm, good." They drove off and took the long way by the ravine where by now small crocuses could be seen, something that always thrilled her. But Greg paid no attention to the flowers. "I got tickets for the Sunday game," he told her and she could feel how much he was looking forward to that.

So they talked about the team's chances for the season. Fran knew her baseball all right. That was one side that he had brought out in her and she had learned to yell with the noisiest of fans. "Might be cool on Sunday," she said, "we'll need sweaters maybe. Good that I didn't put them away yet."

They loaded up on foodstuffs and it was fun to go to the store with a man. Why wouldn't Phil ever go? Well. Back home they stuffed the groceries away and then Greg went to fix the gutter on the back roof. She heard the clatter over the Grand Canyon Suite she had put on the record player and the music sounded just right. Greg, that big bear, out there fixing . . . he came back in. "Anything else to fix, hon?" "Fix me and you a drink, that's what you can do." He made her an old fashioned and had a beer for himself.

"Fran," he said, "I want you to read something." Greg went and pulled a magazine out of his briefcase. No, of course, it wasn't poetry, that was not Greg. It was an article on the gathering of wild rice in the marshes of Northern Minnesota. Greg had some Indian blood in him and there was some identification with Indians which he held up to Fran almost as if to say, "See, kid, I'm really a wild Indian. Can you take it? Can you take me?" She took it fine and laughed over the whole rice business. She promised to read the article but was surprised that Greg had taken to reading the *New Yorker*. He guessed what she was thinking and said, "You know I don't read this kind of stuff usually, but somebody pointed it out to me." They talked a bit about this and that, one thing leading to another. Wild rice led to the film, *Bitter Rice*, to the starving people in the south to Greg's work which kept him informed about economic conditions all over the world. This was always fascinating to Fran. With Greg she felt engaged with the whole globe. So that brought out atlases and maps and she learned how the lira stood and how banking started in Italy. They had a book on Florence and when they paged through it they found a picture of a guy who looked a lot like Phil to her. She quickly went on to another page and Greg never noticed. "We ought to go to Florence. We must, we must."

"Careful now," Fran said as he kissed her and he was. And then there was morning, and then there were other mornings. On one of them, she woke with a fever. Greg took over, cancelled appointments at the office, called the doctor, took her temperature, changed the sheets, fed her pills, read to her, closed the curtains, wiped the sweat from her forehead and other places, and heard her breathe easier again when she got better. He scolded her for not having a tidier medicine closet. He couldn't find a damn thing. Fran promised to reform, only to mutter to herself, "What's the difference?" When she was better she asked if she had been talking in her fever, afraid of having said things that perhaps would—"You talked about filter cigarettes, you dummy," Greg said. Fran smiled.

She was well again. They discussed her taking a job. She had been a crack private secretary and their latest discussions convinced her that she was getting stagnant, rotting on the vine, and she longed for involvement with real moving matters again. Greg was against it. He didn't want her to complicate her life. "But dear, there is no complication. I am drying up here. I need to feel in touch with things going on. I'll be the better for it at home, believe me." In the end he gave in reluctantly. Then he went to work on it. Made some contacts for her. Drove her to the interview and finally was proud of her; she had latched onto a good job with an electronics firm.

They celebrated by going out to eat enormous steaks and he persuaded her to try beer once more. Once more she tried it and once more she disliked it. Greg flirted with the waitress, but she didn't mind. Greg gave the waitress an enormous tip, but she didn't mind. Greg called the waitress honey, but she didn't mind. But she tried to get out of the restaurant quickly because all of a sudden she couldn't stand Greg being so hearty and good humored. She wanted to get away and she got away to a fantasy that had Phil sitting on the porch whittling away at a piece of ash—no, not that, and she blushed. So she snuggled against Greg in the car, hungry now for getting him to her—yes, to and into. Greg was there. That's what counted.

A New Today

The preceding episode was designed to tax the reader's fantasy. In following Vicky and Jim or Greg and Fran through these few pages, it is easy to imagine oneself in their kitchens, in their yards, in their beds, and their bathrooms—trying on their skins and feeling what they might have felt, or perhaps playing out the role of the other spouses: Jim's other wife, Ann, or Fran's other husband, Phil.

That, of course, is what I made up: two polygamous relationships. My invention is characterized by a great number of simplifications and I shall not explain away reality. Let me elaborate on what I have taken for granted so as to make it possible for us to observe our principles, Vicky, Jim, Fran and Greg, *in situ*.

1. Our couples are living in a society which has engineered a transition from monogomous to polygamous marriage, legalized it through appropriate laws, and set up an appropriate financial support system; as we tune in on our couples we find them living in an era perhaps a generation or two removed from the establishment of the polygamous system. A single standard is now in existence offering both men and women opportunities to be married to more than one spouse. The mores have caught up to a large degree with the changes now, and with the support of religious philosophies as well as new ethical codes, our married pairs are living their lives polygamously together with millions of other such couples. The society leaves the choice up to the individuals. Men and women have no moral scruples about the polyandrous or polygenous arrangement; they discuss the scruples of their grandparents in historical terms, as a curious stage in the development of the family system. They have learned in sociology classes that previous generations shook their heads when scientists photographed copulating couples for research purposes, or when spouses chose partners for a night or a fortnight to whom they were not married.

In the new era, it is taken for granted that both men and women want variety in their relationships, a variety not diminishing the quality and richness of the person, but yielding more experiences and bringing out different facets of oneself, a variety enabling people to affirm themselves more fully, to actualize themselves more powerfully. In this new era individuals look with an almost condescending smile upon the earlier period in which, seemingly, the standard assumption was that one could love only one person at a time, while, in fact, most people love more than one person anyway. But their teachers point out that it was exactly the dissatisfaction with the tentativeness of pseudo-monogamy which lead to the social change when the society at large accepted polygamy. At the time of these "stories" there are still pockets of resistance left, but for the most part, public discussion pro and con has ceased.

The two couples live in an industrial society unlike the other polygamous ones, Mormon or Muslim. While members of this society acknowledge kinship to their polygamous cousins of yesteryear, they consider themselves participants in a new phase of history. They are still somewhat self-conscious, at least on occasions when they are face to face with family history, the picture albums, and the keepsakes. But it is not a strong emotion.

It is easy to see, then, why I have not placed the two pairs in a specific decade or century.

2. Another area of simplification concerns children and in-laws. It is obvious that a society which established polygamy had to deal with and to resolve questions regarding the legality of offspring and the creation of new inheritance regulations; by the second or third generation a climate was produced in which these children could accept their origin no matter who had fathered them. What about the mothers? How would they use their children as leverage on husbands in these multiple relationships and, conversely, how would fathers learn to deal with emotions toward their own children, children from different co-spouses? There are emotional attachments to be dealt with. Feelings of belonging, loyalty, and pride would arise and must be reckoned with, particularly if children by different husbands lived in the same household.

And then kin. The pulls of married pairs by their parents is a universal phenomenon. In a polygamous system, these pulls are multiplied and proliferated. It can be understood now why in my story of Fran and Greg, Vicky and Jim, neither children nor parents populate the scene.

3. The third and most important consideration is that in each of the two situations described, the two different spouses are residing in separate households though they live in the same geographical area. The relationships are thus unencumbered by the complexities which must arise when co-spouses live under the same roof with their mate, two wives with one husband or two husbands with one wife. Even in that setup alternate living arrangements are possible. Separate quarters could be maintained, even in the same house. But it also seems likely that arrangements are possible in which all three would occupy the same room, even bedroom, if not even bed.

The reality of such *ménage à trois* arrangements could make for openness and certainly prevent pretentiousness (after all, there is always someone else there); it could simplify economic and financial matters. It might, however, present at least two sets of problems which I can only touch on here. First, of course, is possible competitiveness. While the polygamous arrangement removes the equation, "Not to be the only one diminishes me as a person," and there is no fear of having to be replaced, it is likely that the wish to be number one in the affection and attention of the spouse will remain. One is likely to compare one's qualities with the qualities of the co-spouse even when that co-spouse is not really a rival, and even if it is accepted that one was chosen in the first place for one's differentness from the co-spouse.

Under the same roof these differences in personality and character are constantly on view and there is ample opportunity to experience the interplay of these psychological and emotional reactions of the other two engaged in some social or menial activity. Having postulated differences in the co-spouses and consequent competitiveness between them, I would advance that there would be less competitiveness if the spouses were similar. But to establish a household with similar co-spouses seems absurd in light of the fact that the system was founded in the first place to provide for variety. Vicky and Ann, Greg and Phil, knowing of each other's existence, nevertheless have minimal information about each other—which could make for either more or less competitiveness. At this time I don't know which it might be. Social psychological research might eventually provide an answer.

Secondly, let us take a look at how the spouse to the co-spouses manages. Having the co-spouses in different households makes for maximum compartmentalization which I feel is necessary for the system to work. In order to relate to a co-spouse there should be as few reminders about the other co-spouse as possible and the question is, *How possible is that?* In the anecdotes above, there seems to be a good deal of "contamination." At what point compartmentalization breaks down is hard to predict, but I would believe that a constant influx of memories about the other and a comparison with a non-present co-spouse would make a relationship confusing, disturbing, and unsatisfactory. Co-spouses under the same roof, of course, could be appreciated for what they both bring to the relationship, but at the same time? *Ménage à trois* permanent households would make heavy demands on the social, intellectual, emotional, and sexual powers of the principal spouse even though the co-spouses would meet an array of needs for him (her) that would be extremely satisfying.

This brings up yet another point which I took for granted. I described these couples as rather vague personalities. Certain characteristics were stressed, to be sure, but the real question is what personality types will be suitable for a polygamous arrangement. Without going into personality theory here, I can suggest, however, that the polygamous arrangements might be more possible for "sophisticated" types. Yet this kind of classification may have little utility in a society which I described earlier, in which polygamy is a legal and social option. Such a system might also seriously change the dimensions of what we now call psychopathy or sociopathy. (This category now includes behaviors which in the polygamous system have been institutionalized.) Along more subtle personal lines, however, what about privacy, for instance, in *ménage à trois* living arrangements? Would one predict that persons who are protective of their privacy would be unlikely candidates for a co-spouse arrangement?

Another problem regards mobility. To transfer one's life to another community is a common expectation among Americans. To move two households and their combined attachments is another complication unless, of course, the three spouses are living in widely separated geographical areas anyway.

I really made it rather simple for Vicky and Jim, and for Greg and Fran. If they have really succeeded with their relationships it is as a result of having managed all of the problems mentioned in my discussion. Seemingly, the price to pay for marrying two wives or husbands and thus availing oneself of marital variety, is making one's own life enormously complex. I have given each spouse only two co-spouses, and I shall leave it to the reader's imagination as to what complexities would be introduced by adding additional co-spouses. Only those who can deal effectively with complexity can make polygamy work for them.

HERBERT A. OTTO

10

The New Marriage:
Marriage as a Framework
for Developing Personal Potential[1]

Introduction

It is currently the assumption of many leading behavioral scientists (Abraham Maslow, Margaret Mead, Gardner Murphy, Carl Rogers, and Gordon Allport) that the average healthy human being is functioning at a fraction of his capacity. We often hear that the productive person of today is functioning at 10 percent of his ability. Margaret Mead quotes a 6 percent figure, and my own estimate is closer to 5 percent.[2, 3, 4]

If we accept this hypothesis, the actualizing of our potential can become the most exciting adventure of our lifetime. Conversely, if we do not use our energies in a continuous process of self-realization and personal growth, the very same energies are directed into destructive channels. If we do not employ these energies positively to actualize our potential, the energies are "short-circuited" and become destructive to the organism as a whole. *In the not-too-distant future, we will discover that there is nothing more destructive to the human personality than the damming, blocking, and shutting off of the processes associated with ongoing personality growth and the actualizing of personal potential.*

[1] This Chapter is a revision of an address delivered at the 1969 Convention of the California Personnel and Guidance Association, Anaheim, California.

[2] Herbert A. Otto, *ed.*, *Explorations in Human Potentialities* (Springfield, Ill., Charles C. Thomas, 1966).

[3] Herbert A. Otto, *Guide to Developing Your Potential* (New York, Charles Scribner's Sons, 1967).

[4] Herbert A. Otto, *ed.*, *Human Potentialities: The Challenge and The Promise* (St. Louis, Warren H. Green, 1968).

The lack of commitment to self-realization, together with the lack of framework and opportunity for self-realization, are responsible for much of what is labeled as pathological or asocial behavior, "acting out," etc. Actually, this type of symptomatology must be understood as a symbolic form of communication and is really a cry for help. It is a type of flailing about and seeking of change to the best of the person's ability at that time and moment in his life space. The very anger and hostility that such behavior arouses in us is a very clear indication that the individual is still fighting, that he is still attempting to actualize and has not given up his efforts. I am far more concerned about the vast segments of our population who have, in a sense, given up on life. These people live in quiet desperation, believing themselves trapped, yet fearing to leave the comfort of their entrapment. Most tragically, *they do not know that they have a potential to actualize*, and, therefore, they have little reason to hope.

We must begin to reach this segment of our society which feels relatively hopeless, is committed to the *status quo*, is dulled by routine, and permeated by boredom. We must reach them with our human potentiality concepts and with opportunities to actualize their potential. It is especially important to reach out to this segment of our society because they form a reservoir of hate and destructiveness which may well set off an epidemic of hate. Yet this reservoir of hatred does offer a dynamic opportunity for social change and regeneration, for by channeling this energy toward the development of individual abilities and talents and the actualizing of personal potential, leadership is thereby created which can then be applied to the regeneration of our social institutions and structures.

Our societal structures and institutions have a great influence on what we call "personality" and the dimensions of our human functioning. The actualizing of our human potential is closely bound to the regeneration of our human institutions. As always, *we must begin with ourselves and the institutions with which we are most intimately concerned and connected*. Those of us who are married can begin with an assessment of the institution we call marriage.

If two partners envision their marriage as a framework for actualizing personal potential, the following key question becomes pertinent: "Are both partners satisfied with their rate of personal growth while engaged in this ongoing relationship we call marriage?" All too often, marriage results in a dull, stultifying routine, deadly to the growth processes of both marital partners. Many times, boredom and satiation with each other is made tolerable largely by the devotion and responsibilities attendant to the upbringing of the children. The three ingredients of such a marriage, which are the children, habit, and fear of social stigma, form an unhealthy glue, when it is the *only* glue which keeps a marriage together. There are more such marriages than we would care to admit. This is the tremendous clinical substratum of "indifferent" or "tolerable" marriages. This type of marriage unfortunately never reaches the counselor, but contributes to massive unhappiness, discontent, and finally the utter capitulation of a life endured, but not lived joyously.

Conversely, marriage can be envisioned as a framework for actualizing personal potential. *The concepts, approaches, and methods which have been the outgrowth of research in the area of Human Potentialities can revitalize marriage as an institution.* In a large number of instances, where marriage ends in a divorce, one or both partners, consciously or unconsciously, recognize that the nature of the relationship has become progressively inimical to their personality growth and actually impedes, or is destructive to, the actualizing of personal potential. In contrast, the New Marriage offers an ongoing adventure of self-discovery, personal growth, unfoldment, and fulfillment. Growth by its very nature is not smooth or easy, for growth involves change and the emergence of the new. But growth and the actualizing of personal potential is also a joyous and deeply satisfying process which can bring to marriage a new quality of zest for living, of joie de vivre, and of excitement.

The New Marriage: Some Dimensions and Characteristics

There are a number of dimensions and characteristics which, in the aggregate, form a unique Gestalt and distinguish the New Marriage from contemporary marriage patterns.

1. *There is clear acknowledgment by both partners concerning the personal relevance of the Human Potentialities hypothesis: that the healthy individual is functioning at a fraction of his potential.*

This hypothesis is not yet widely known and is still restricted to a relatively small percentage of the population, mostly to the group with a college education. And, to most of those who are acquainted with the

Human Potentialities hypothesis, it remains an idle fact, to be filed away in the storehouse of knowledge. There is no awareness that this datum is personally relevant and should be, or is, leading to personal involvement and action designed to develop potential.

2. *Love and understanding become dynamic elements in the actualization of the marital partners' personal potential.*

Love and understanding become strong supportive forces which encourage and sustain the marital partners in their commitment to self-unfoldment and personal growth. Both partners are aware that there are methods and approaches available, designed to deepen understanding and strengthen the love relationship. They utilize these techniques to bring their love to fuller flowering, to deepen and expand the affectional flow, and to expand the quality of their understanding. Utilizing their love and understanding, both partners foster and support each other's efforts to become more self-actualizing human beings. They help each other to help themselves. To use contemporary language, in the New Marriage, the two persons are devoted to turning each other on and this turns them on.

3. *Both partners in the New Marriage are interested in, and participate in, ongoing growth groups, or groups designed to help them to actualize personal potential.*

There is recognition that "we grew into what we are through relationships with people; we grow into what we can be through relationships with people." Husband and wife seek those group experiences which they feel will help them to grow as persons. They are involved in both ongoing group experiences, as well as in individual experiences designed to actualize their personal potential. If possible, they will verbally share these experiential encounters with their marital partner. Currently there are over eighty Growth Centers in the United States, similar to Esalen Institute and Kairos Institute, both in California. (*See* Appendix for a list of growth centers.) This recent development is often referred to as the Human Potentialities Movement. Growth Centers offer ongoing group experiences, weekend marathons, and seminars led by professionals (psychologists, psychiatrists, counselors, social workers, etc.), all of which are designed to help participants actualize more of their possibilities. The Humanistic psychologists have played a strong role in the genesis of this movement. A very large range of exciting new methods and approaches are available, and new ones are constantly developed. The movement represents the growing edge in the exploration of man's inner universe and the realization of his powers.

4. *There is clear recognition by both partners that personality and the actualizing of human potential have much to do with the social institutions and structures within which man functions. The need for institutional regeneration is acknowledged by both partners as being personally relevant, leading to involvement in social action.*

The husband and wife of the New Marriage recognize that social concern and social responsibility must lead to their involvement as change agents in the local institutions of which they are a member or in which they participate. They know that by the exercise of social responsibility through action, they develop their leadership potential and that this has an effect on the development of other latent abilities and capacities. They realize that to achieve the regeneration of our society we must examine our institutions in the light of the following question: "To what extent does the function of the institution foster the realization of human potential?"

5. *There is clear awareness by husband and wife that their interpersonal or relationship environment as well as their physical environment directly affects the actualization of individual potential.*

The husband and wife together examine their acquaintanceship and friendship circle with the aim of seeking closer relationships with those people who stimulate them, encourage them, and enhance either partner's creativity. They seek to deepen and extend friendship relations and to seek out new people who, by the nature of their being, provide growth experiences. Husband and wife keep their home environment dynamic, both supporting and reflecting their own growth and change. Both partners recognize that the pollution of the air that we breathe, the water we drink and swim in, and the plundering and spoiling of our natural resources and wilderness areas is for the profit of the few and to the detriment of the many. They become involved in action to help shape a physical environment favorable to man's development.

6. *The New Marriage is Here-and-Now oriented and not bound to the past.*

More important than the past history of the marriage is what the partners wish to do in the Here-and-Now to accomplish change and growth. Emphasis is on employment of the will and on the utilization of growth processes. A marriage is not its past, but what both partners envision it can be, and what they are willing to invest to make it so.

7. *Partners in the New Marriage conceive of their union as an evolving, developing, flexible institution.*

Both partners together decide what is right for them, and in a very real sense, they determine the dimensions, structures, and function of their marriage. This is an ongoing process, with changes determined both by individual growth needs and by helping to unfold and actualize each other. There is recognition that the New Marriage is a flexible framework which may lead to other structures of togetherness. There is ongoing commitment to experimental living, to seeking of new experiences, to providing for new inputs. Most importantly, emphasis is placed on the development of a life-affirmative, positive attitude. Joy and pleasure are placed in the service of unfolding the individual's potential. There is a strong focus on joy as an important component of living and on joy as a creative experience. There is an emphasis on the cultivation of ecstasy and on the joyous celebration of life.

8. *Husband and wife have an interest in exploring the spiritual dimensions of the New Marriage.*

Both partners explore in depth the relationship of their value and belief structure *vis-à-vis* their marriage. They examine the relationship of values and beliefs to their functioning inside and outside of the marriage —they live as they believe. They explore and develop spiritual dimensions in their sexual relationship. They discover how their involvement in religious organizations can regenerate these structures. They seek to deepen their understanding of God, the Godhead, or the Universe.

9. *In the New Marriage, there is planned action and commitment to achieve realization of marriage potential.*

The concept of "marriage potential" means that in every marriage there is a potential for greater happiness, for increased productivity, creativity, enjoyment, communication, for more love, understanding, and warmth. Since it is often difficult for two people to actualize more of their marriage potential by themselves, participants in the New Marriage will seek out group experiences designed to deepen their relationship and functioning as a couple. Such experiences are now being offered at many of the Growth Centers.

If we conceive of the New Marriage as an exciting union which has as its main purpose the involvement of both partners in the adventure of actualizing each other's potential, then this purpose becomes a dynamic bond which fosters closeness while at the same time it meets the privacy needs of the partners. Implicit in the concept of the New Marriage is a deep respect for each other as a unique person with many individual capacities, talents, powers, and abilities which can be developed and brought to full flowering.

Also implicit is the concept that two parents who, in love and understanding, are dedicated to help each other actualize individual potential, are thereby doing more for the family than the heads of a child-centered marriage, where the efforts of the parents are subordinated to the needs of the children. The family devoted to the actualizing of the personal potential of its members provides necessary structure, as well as the freedom of group experiences, for growth as a family and individual growth experiences away from the family. These experiences are consciously designed and worked out by the family as a group, with primary emphasis on the needs and the wishes of the individuals involved. The actualization of a member's potential is first and foremost his own concern, but it is also the concern of the other family members who encourage, help, and assist. The primary emphasis, however, is on the individual's efforts to help himself. From this emphasis emerges a new freedom within the structure, and this marks the emergence of *The New Family*.

Much of what happens (or what doesn't happen) in a contemporary marriage is determined by the implicit assumptions underlying the union. Some of these change during a marriage, others do not. To a considerable extent, *these underlying assumptions define the course of the marriage and provide a framework which shapes the nature of the relationship.* Some of these assumptions are verbalized at some time during the marriage while others are rarely, if ever, put into words. Among these assumptions are:

1. Marriage furnishes a means for the giving and taking of love, understanding, and for sexual fulfillment.

2. Sexual relations should take place only (or largely) between the two partners.

3. Marriage offers a measure of security, comfort, and stability, so that both partners soon learn to know what they can expect. Boundaries are set by husband and wife and it is their expectation that these will be respected.

4. Marriage involves a set of responsibilities and duties. It also involves certain roles—"what a husband is and should be" and "what a wife is and should be."

5. Marriage is for the raising and rearing of children and "having a family."

6. Marriage is a means of "weathering life's storms and ups-and-downs."

7. Marriage means companionship, someone to talk to.

8. Marriage is an insurance against a lonely old age.

In a similar manner, the implicit and explicit assumptions underlying the New Marriage will determine its course. For this reason, a New Marriage must begin with an exploration of these assumptions by both marital partners. As husband and wife enter into this process, openness and self-disclosure lead to increased personal authenticity and the emergence of a deeper understanding and vital togetherness. The concept of the New Marriage can offer new opportunities, open new doors, and add new creativity, excitement, and joy to married living.

11

The Tribal Family
and the Society of Awakening

The Tribal Family as such is a phenomenon of the 1960's, this decade during which evolution of social experiences accelerated to revolutionary tempo. A joining of fantasy and experimentation to an exuberant life energy repressed during the fifties pushed aside unrewarding inter-personal patterns and recklessly aimed for a new Society of Awakening.[1] Pre-existing patterns of life behavior fractured like glacial ice under the impact of technological changes such as increases in mobility afforded by the automobile and airplane; traditional family units split and dissolved under the impact of divorce or geographic and vocational mobility. The long-existing Western emphasis on individual freedom resulted in value changes toward determination of mores and morality by individual rather than family. This trend was reinforced by the removal of certain disagreeable consequences of spontaneous sexual behavior through the cure of disease and the development of chemical means of contraception. Affluence for middle-class members of American society made comfortable subsistence with a minimum of work feasible, although generally socially envied and disapproved of by the strongly persistent Puritan ethos. Intellectual inquiry joined to psychoanalytically-generated emotional striving towards evolving new methods of personal satisfaction and security, sought to find new role relationships providing intimate gratifications not ordinarily found in contemporary families.

[1] A term I have chosen as preferable to "hippy." It is used as in the quotation: "... like the word 'awakening'—something encouraging and compelling, consoling and full of promise." Herman Hesse in *Magister Ludi* (New York, Holt, Rinehart & Winston, 1968).

For this society of awakening three values stand out: re-examination of traditional socially-inculcated patterns and values through direct experience; a deep mistrust of unverified authority; and joy in living. (Life is for experiencing fully *now*, rather than at a postponed future date.)

A different, although not necessarily new, family form is developing spontaneously through direct life experience. More commonly non-reflective and informal than the product of exhaustive analysis and reflective discussion, this new family form appeals most strongly to the mobile, youthful, white middle-class, who remember the security of a three generation supportive family unit and yet have experienced in their own life-times the disruption and isolation springing from their parents' depression-generated preoccupation with "getting ahead," gaining material satisfactions, security, and the social status of power and conspicuous consumption. Negroes are few, very few, in this awakening society—theirs is a harder and more pitiless world leaving no room for self-exploration or such gentle arts as meditation. The ghetto Negro knows and tolerates the hippy as a next door neighbor, one of the few ghetto-living whites; awakening culture modes (music, art, the wearing of beads) are now seen in the ghettos.

A prominent personal historical characteristic common among tribal family members is a childhood emotional isolation associated with a wistful seeking to gain love and security in a new kinship system. They try to reconstitute the loving, accepting, undemanding family unit which either was lost or never existed at all. The tribal family members act out a Camelot-like legend, seeking a brotherhood and sisterhood of sharing, loving, and growing. Sadly, they often frustrate their own yearnings through naivete, inexperience, or lack of discipline. Their expressed social ideal is that of equality of all members in a freely giving, freely receiving cooperative; their reality is different, ranging from traditional tribal systems headed by the Old Man or the Mother; to fairly stable, hardworking cooperatives: to loose peer-groups of limited duration cohabiting in one dwelling; to isolated anarchic fear-laden situations similar to Golding's novel, *The Lord of the Flies*.

The term "tribe" has traditionally connoted a stable group membership, usually partially of blood kin, having historical continuity. Our contemporary "tribal" relationship does not meet these criteria. Today's tribal groups are persons usually not blood kin (other than children) who have a semipermanent economic, sexual, and dwelling relationship on the basis of common needs and interests. The interests may be artistic, economic, productive, social-sexual, or ideologic. In any case, tribal family members seek the security of becoming "insiders" by association with like-minded persons. We are not dealing with a basically new social phenomena in this restitutive grouping response of socially dissatisfied or isolated single persons. As in past times, we are seeing persons seeking the necessary security and gratification of association with others, by coalescing around the simplest of traditional human group structures, the tribe. Certain unique features do characterize the evolving tribal family of the present day, in contrast to the roving bands of children who foraged for themselves in the desolation of Russia after the First World War, or the highly successful Oneida Colony which flourished in upper New York State in the nineteenth century. For example, the tribal family of today is primarily an urban phenomena, although certain forces do tend to move it out into rural areas.

I have not found a satisfactory way to examine objectively from a socio-psychological viewpoint human relationships so in flux. The families I know at close range vary from so-called "intentional communities" founded upon certain basic relationship propositions which then determine both family form and function (for example, meditation as the way to revelation, commonality of sexual partners or vegetarianism) to spontaneous and usually shortlived congeries of persons come together by chance for mutual protection and satisfaction. The longest-lived of these novel forms generally have at least two of the following three characteristics: first, foundation on pre-existing conventional family structure which extends into the non-conventional tribal family; second, a definite and acknowledged leader having major authority; and third, a clear economic function, such as operation of a business or resort.

Intermediate between the conventional family and the tribal family is the divorce-evolved extended family. The legal pattern or the socially-sanctioned pattern of marriage relationships has changed radically throughout the United States in the past two generations. In California particularly, the high incidence of divorce and remarriage amounts to widespread serial polygamy. Thus, a legally-sanctioned form of extended family has developed. The realistic needs of child care split between biological parents living at separate residences, the network of socially-mandated economic relationships in the form of child support and alimony, and the usually battered but often still effective emotional ties between former marriage partners, have all resulted in large numbers of middle-class children having relationships to three, four and more family groups. Parents, step-parents, and married older siblings all act in parental roles. The children involved in such matings, unmatings, and rematings become accustomed to a number of often disjunctive parental relationships which must be resolved by the adaptability of the child. A tribal situation thus evolves. In many of these multiple, legal, family life situations, the parents act on a loose yet effectively coherent system of standards and values. While these more conventional extended families will not be considered in this discussion, recognize that at times the legally-sanctioned progressive polygamy of the divorce court leads directly into the non-legally sanctioned yet socially condoned relationships of the so-called tribal family.

Certain tribal family characteristics need to be itemized. As mentioned previously, the tribal family is a feature of the diffusely evolving subculture I call the "Society of Awakening." The type of most current interest and notoriety is the so-called "Hippie" tribal family, which is often characterized by youth, instability of membership, open nonconformity, and energy. Generally their values are the following:

1. *They seek to gain spontaneity and freedom from the internalized conventional middle-class social conditioning they consider individually inhibiting and self-frustrating.* (This is called "de-imprinting.")

2. *Self-perfection and growth are then to be achieved through establishing self-chosen behavior standards after this release from the conventional social structure and demands.* This process leads to a re-evaluation of the usual middle-class standards on social relationships of all types. This would include: limitation of sexual partners to legally-approved monogamous, face-to-face genital intercourse; cleanliness; the value of "legal" marriage and child legitimacy; the sanctification of work; the necessity for frugality and money saving; future orientation rather than present orientation; the attainment of socially-valued status signs (particularly those of conspicuous material consumption such as clothing and automobiles) and of visible social power attainments (credit cards, executive positions, belonging to the "right" club, etc.). These are all re-examined *through experience* and fitting patterns for the individual are determined. For example, one "hippy" household of seven people is as "square" (conventional) as square can be regarding marriage and sexual partners; they regard work as having a high

spiritual value. They also believe in educating their children to their own values and have formed a school emphasizing meditation, frugality, folk art, and vegetarianism.

3. *There is self-preoccupation, and an insistent emphasis that the right of the individual to determine his or her own conduct must have a high priority over the demands of the social group in general.* The usual limits on this are non-violence, non-exploitation of others, and lack of coercion. As shame, as well as the allied viewing and touching taboos, is generally absent in the Awakening Society, the grounds for offending others are far less than in the general society.

4. *Membership in the tribal family is generally dependent upon full acceptance of any newcomer by all mature members of the community.* The newcomer's role and the method of entry will make some difference, of course. If a new woman is relating to a male member who has no "old lady" (recognized monogamous relationship), the tendency will be to accept the new woman. If an unattached newcomer accepts a recognized subordinate role to the existing women in the community until such a time as trial probation of an informal sort is over, she too can become an acknowledged member of the female side of the clan.

5. *There is a re-differentiation of man-woman roles which runs counter to the prevailing diffusion of sexual roles in our current technological society.* As has been pointed out frequently, in the suburban two-generation family (which is now becoming the middle-class norm) husband-wife roles in terms both of money-earning and child-rearing have tended to blur. There is an increasing number of wives in the middle-class labor market concomitant with a decrease in specific functional family role of the husband. In the tribal families, while both sexes work, women are generally in a service role, such as waitress, masseuse, and secretary. Male dominance is held desirable by both sexes. The recognized dress is in a semi-rural or western style which emphasizes sexual differences. The women tend to wear long dresses and long hair, while the men tend toward the western or frontier clothing of boots, rough-woven cloths, and outdoor jackets. Both men and women in their feasts and celebrations will combine this western mode with the currently déclassé "hippy" styles imported from Carnaby Street in England.

6. *The Puritan middle-class premium on work as sanctification in both the secular and sacred worlds is largely absent, with a playing down of the importance of the work relationship.* The extent of this work

de-emphasis varies between family groups. Some family groups are formed as work-centered groups and members are expected to contribute labor or money. If they do not contribute, there will be a formal or informal re-evaluation of their family roles, the decision being whether or not they should be permitted to stay.

The value system in regard to gainful employment is to try to maintain as close an association between work and the living situation as possible. To this end, artistic cooperatives based on a tribal family living style are numerous. Music and public entertainment groups such as the "Family Dog," based in San Francisco, are spreading throughout cities of the West. Groups developed to operate resort and "creative living" centers have been established.

This awakening society expresses revulsion at the high degree of separation in the general American culture between the individual's work, and recreational activity and the family life sphere. They hold that the individual cannot be integrated within himself or his family group if his life pattern is fragmented. They point to the fact that the father in the average suburban family works far from the home, and that the relationship between home and office is often one of tension and competition for his time. A great deal of the family life is taken up with being transported; the husband commutes, the wife chauffeurs constantly from school to business to club to special tutoring and so forth; the children bus to and from school. So, in the Society of Awakening, another principle of the tribal families is conscious integration and harmony of all aspects of life. To this end, the close integration of work with the daily living patterns represents both a matter of convenience in earning a living, and an attitude toward the working environment as identical to other elements of total life space.

7. *The families are to all intents and purposes communal living situations such as those of much older intentional communities.* (The aforementioned Oneida Community is related in this feature to the religiously-based fraternal orders of the traditional Christian Churches, the Dukhobors of Canada, and the Hutterites of Canada and the United States.) Properties are held in common, with a strong basic attitude that property rights are subordinate to human needs. One prominent characteristic of the families is their tradition of warm hospitality both to known friends of the extended family and to the well-disposed stranger. The best-publicized aspect of this particular trait is that of the "Diggers," a West Coast movement which has spread to

the East Coast. This loose organization, which does not in general qualify as a tribal family although in certain cities it may function on this basis (i.e., San Francisco's Happening House) exists to provide without charge the necessities of life to persons in need.

8. *Social responsibility is of great importance.* This particular functional evolution of the larger aspect of the "hippy" or Awakening Society is worthy of a paper in itself. Briefly, the society or subculture of the Awakened is constantly meeting with large numbers of new persons of all ages entering from the middle-class who are not equipped realistically to meet the basic problems of living. These volunteers or self-nominees for the process of Awakening have been crippled in life-competence, partly by a monstrous social and pedagogical over-emphasis on information recording and retrieval. As is generally acknowledged, this information drilled into them in school has little relevance to real here-and-now life. The entire personality-warping process has functional value only for advancement in the academic nether-world and its related business and military domains. Under the name of "Diggers" (in Cromwellian times, a group who fed the poor by digging the public meadows into gardens) there spontaneously sprung up an organization taking from the wasted surplus of the general American society discarded (sometimes contributed) goods which could maintain these socially-crippled newcomers. Without any prodding beyond the realities of life in the streets, and supported marginally by the sharing of more adapted social members, these middle-class social infants learn life's realities through direct experience. By evolutionary retraining, some few awaken to become stable members of a society aimed at growth and the realization of innate unique potential, rather than remaining confined to narrow socially-enforced work specialization. The larger majority return to their middle-class homes, perhaps half awake.

9. *Each tribal family develops within itself sexual patterns which are suited to that particular group's needs and goals.* While the general society condemns (and envies) "hippy" or Awakening Society as "sexually promiscuous," erotic sex is less conspicuous here than in the larger world. There are certain tribal families, for example, which are based upon severe limitation of sexual partners and a general rechanneling of the erotic impulse through sublimation. Complete sexual abstinence on ethical grounds is not unknown. Sexual mores and behavior are much more open and acknowledged than the sexual mores of existing middle-class society; prurient titillation, curiosity, and shame are

uncommon. In existing, sanctioned middle-class society there is a large amount of extra-marital erotic sensual behavior, both that leading to direct sexual intercourse and of the so-called "flirtation" type. Among the Awakened there is much less, although this varies widely from group to group. As a general rule, there is recognized and tacitly accepted extra-marital sensuality (including genital eroticism) as well as pre- and post-marital sensuality. In the families such behavior is explicitly recognized, although the mode in which it is expressed may vary widely. Certain intentional communities are based upon an amplification of sexual behavior to a group norm which values orgasm (of a generalized rather than a solely genital type) as a primary life occupation. In other situations, all mature adult members of the community are held in common. Lastly is the more casual situation in which each member of the community is free to establish whatever relationships are desired with any other adult member of the community. (This is a model exemplified in *Stranger in a Strange Land* by Heinlein.) Interestingly enough, homoeroticism is uncommon in the tribal family, although certainly not unknown. Where homoeroticism exists, it is generally a secondary sexual "outlet," as defined by Kinsey and Associates, with the primary outlet being heterosexual.

Tribal family members, mainly under thirty years of age, have a much greater sexual interest and expression than recognized in our general social "norms." Legal sexual "norms" in conventional society are set by the older members of the community, and codified into laws enacted generally by sexually-quiescent men fifty or older, who utilize values and standards set in their childhoods. Due to the diminished sexual needs and obsolescent social standards of these older persons, the normative behaviors and the legal standards set by them are ludicrously inappropriate for a youthful, sexually virile population. Mitigating the stringency of such sexual laws is the laxity of their enforcement. The law lags behind social attitude, which has been changed by the Freudian revolution. No longer is violent repression considered the most desirable social mode of dealing with instinctual drives. Admittedly, some legislators and governors prefer force to self-examination and re-education; nonetheless, expression is usually considered preferable to repression. This more optimal course has led cautiously to a more open acknowledgment of, if not a greater general participation in, sexual activities.

In the Awakening Society, particularly within impromptu and

generally transitory beginner family groups based upon a common dwelling (an apartment in the Village, or in Haight-Ashbury) there is a considerable frequency of sexual expression, in the form of heterosexual intercourse on a casual basis. Among older groups, however, there is a marked preponderance of men over women, creating, in effect, a system of polyandry for several of the women, although others may have essentially monogamous relationships. As experience is gained by newcomers, this sexual "spree" generally gives way to the quiet, semi-permanent, monogamous relationship characteristic of many in our general society. The adolescent beginner matures from sexual and social rebellion into a self-aware, enlightened, self-choosing, adjusting rather than defying, adult. The generally quiet, peaceful attitude and lack of tension, noteworthy characteristics of the mature "awakened" adult in the tribal families, are associated with conscious avoidance of general life tension. (Their term: "I don't get hassled.") Specifically erotic tension is released through frequent erotic sexuality.[2] Frequent sexuality is much facilitated by the association of work and family situation, as there is little of the conventional emphasis on routinized set hours of work activity during which sexual activity is considered not only inappropriate but almost immoral. "Love" in all its beautiful, physical, emotional, and spiritual aspects is sought and freely expressed with the least inhibition possible.

From the standpoint of functional changes in families, the "up-tight" nature of the middle-class American family is associated with the diminished amount of sexual gratification available to family members under the present life situations. Although the middle-class intellectually condones sexuality as a gratifying and (in order to be Puritanically acceptable) a "healthful" and "legitimate" life activity, the conditions of middle-class life, with its taboo on open serious discussion of sexual techniques and behavior, inexperience in gratification and limited modes of sensual outlet, often result in a chronically abnormal, heightened level of sexual and libidinal tension.

10. *The ideal of self-perfection, commonly spoken of as "growth," or "finding my thing," is nearly universal in these families.* A great deal of time is spent talking about various forms of self-understanding or "realization of individual potential," or in analyzing, in a scientific or pseudo-scientific manner, the characters and personal attainments of the

---

[2] Marijuana, a mild sedative and euphoriant, also contributes, of course.

members of the family. Such talk ranges from the necessary exchange of information on individuals commonly called "gossiping," to the use of esoteric systems of personality examinations such as astrology or the Tarot, to the more conventional psychoanalytic jargon of the intellectual middle-class. As persons moving into these families tend to come from a wide variety of backgrounds, though generally intellectual and college-educated middle-class, such discussions are usually a potpourri of current and past intellectual, psychoanalytic, or magical systems.

Freudianism is noteworthily absent, except insofar as Freudian psychology has been incorporated into the *lingua franca* of common discussions. Astrology is probably the most universal system used. Other systems include the Gestalt psychology system of Frederick Perls; the Gurdjieff system; scientology or dianetics; and large numbers of interpersonally-based systems of behavior and therapy lumped under the term "humanistic psychology," as well as various systems borrowed from the Orient such as Yoga, Buddhism, Hinduism, Zen-Buddhism, and so forth. Systems of dance, exercise, music, and diet from all over the world are incorporated into what is increasingly tending to be a rich, turbulent, and immensely creative trial of life concepts of all types in a free marketplace of ideas and practice.

11. *Modification of consciousness through the usual variety of methods is a consistent although not invariant characteristic of the tribal family.* In general the emphasis is on meditation, introspection of the less organized types, nature communion, and religious exercises. The use of consciousness-modifying drugs, both legal and interdicted, is common, yet again by no means universal. In some families a member who wishes to engage in drug use must either leave the family entirely or (more commonly) go elsewhere. In general, however, the Society of Awakening does use the less physiologically damaging drugs such as marijuana and LSD as well as the more physiologically damaging drugs such as alcohol and tobacco. The major brain-damaging drugs, heroin and intravenous methadrine, are used, although condemned.

The psychedelic drugs, particularly LSD-25 but also those of more recent advent such as PCP, MDA, TCP, MMDA, and so forth, generally occupy a large part of the inner experience of the Society of Awakening. As discussed previously, regarding sexuality, the usual pattern is for frequent use of drugs as the individual first enters into the interface between the general American society and the Awakening Society. Customarily, there is much less use of psychedelic drugs after the person has attained insight and become a stabilized member of the subculture. General observations about the frequency and type of subculture drug uses are similar to those of all drugs used in the general American society, that is, of alcohol, amphetamines, barbiturates, and tobacco. Persons recognized as members of stable tribal family groups use the drugs considerably less than individuals still unaffiliated, due either to recent arrival in the society, to personal mental illness and emotional instability, or to other factors.

A book commonly used in Awakening Society orientation is a science-fiction novel entitled *Stranger in a Strange Land* by Robert Heinlein. Although the author is reputed to have denied any intent of portraying a pattern of alternate society, his novel nonetheless has been taken as a prototype on which tribal family groups of the Awakened Society can evolve. This particular novel considers the needs for individual security and growth, release of creative potential, and for the attainment of satisfying spiritual as well as secular goals. Envisioned is a society holding certain property and monies in common, holding sexual partners in common based on individual choice, providing for the communal raising of children, and other features mentioned previously. The second half of this book is definitely recommended to anyone interested in a vivid picture of the values, attitudes, goals, specific organization, and probable outcome of tribal family groups.

A much more consciously programmed picture of alternate family modes is that of Aldous Huxley, in his novel *Island*. This work is less influential than Heinlein's popularly written paperback, but is nevertheless an equally important source for the intellectual basis of the evolutionary family structure of the Society of Awakening. More contemporary than *Stranger in a Strange Land*, *Island* portrays a society composed of collections of adoptive families which coexist with the biological families in order to provide surrogate parents, alternate role models, and life experiences for children. In this, *Island* anticipated the development of the forementioned divorce-generated society of multiple parents and family residential sites.

Recognize that we are dealing with a capsule society, the Society of Awakening, which is a definite subculture. Within the subculture the values discussed already differ from those of the general American society, yet the similarities are far greater than the differences. In general, these values are not revolutionary in nature. Rather, they are evolutionary projections of trends already well under way in all technologically based cultures and, at a less urgent pace, affecting the general society. I refer, of course, to such technological changes as previously cited: increased individual mobility, increased affluence, technological change such as the contraceptive pill, the ascendancy of individual determination of life roles, the faltering competence of traditional authority in our time of great change, and so forth.

In the functioning of the tribal family a high value is put on freedom for the individual to determine his own actions, regardless of his social role. This applies equally to women and men. With the increased number of persons in the tribal family, child rearing becomes less of a strain on any one woman, so that there is a greater tendency for women to have geographic mobility, in the form of taking trips to see friends or relatives. Relaxations of the fierce demand of the middle-class parent for the child to be similar to the parent in style, values, and achievements leads to a greater ease and humor in child rearing, and is considerably less demanding for achievement on the part of the family members. For example, far less importance is attached to whether a woman is a good housekeeper in the television-floorwax-commercials-and-women's-magazine sense. The houses and family "pads" are comfortably cluttered, adequately clean but by no means up to the obsessive middle-class standards of immaculateness. There is much more likely to be incense burning in the living room for pleasure in the scent, than airochem spray in the bathroom to obliterate the odors of excretion.

Another characteristic is that with the decreased clear differentiation of the male-female characteristics in dress and so forth, previously mentioned, there is also a concomitant equality of expectation in the social, economic, and the sexual areas. The women expect sexual gratification as a normal, usually daily activity, an essential part of their life style. Pressure of business and social obligations are not acceptable reasons for sexual neglect by their men.

Status expectations are less among the awakened than in our general technological, achievement-oriented society. The person who wishes to gain high prestige and status in the usual sense is generally viewed as being slightly balmy and still "hung-up." Nonetheless, status striving can be recognized as a definite part of the Awakening Society, as well as of the larger society. The awakened, mature person neither seeks nor rejects status. If exceptional in intellectual and spiritual modes, the person may be considered a "guru." [3] A person who shows ambitions

---

[3] A Hindu term meaning, literally, "wise old one," also, religious teacher.

and wishes to be a leader is discussed and examined by other members of the family group. Indeed, he will be judged by all members of the awakening subculture in terms of whether or not this is "his thing." ("Thing" is a voluntary life choice; "bag" is an involuntary choice.) Should it be held that this activity or striving is a true expression of the person's natural talent there is generally enthusiasm for his course, however status-deriving it may be. Should this drive for status and leadership be seen as residual from the "keeping ahead of the Joneses" orientation, or as a drive for status and power above personal values— two attitudes that characterize the achievement-oriented American society—then the person is generally "put down" or considered to be acting in a neurotic fashion.

This evaluation has come up particularly in terms of the successful and prominent musical family members of the Awakened Society, that is, the rock-and-roll bands such as the "Beatles," the "Jefferson Airplane," the "Rolling Stones," and so forth. (Historically, this general reserve about persons who have attained status stems from the "good old boy" attitude, characteristic of parts of the American small town lower middle-class culture. In small towns there is always ambivalence toward group members who have been conspicuous successes. If the person successfully retains his former group identification, his former tastes and loyalties, and his lower class habits, then he is known as a "good old boy" and given enthusiasm reserved for persons of special and major status. He is a "safe" person, like Tennessee Ernie Ford, or Will Rogers. If, however, with the attainment of power and money the individual ceases to maintain his group identification, he is then considered to be "high-faluting," status-hungry and denying his group of origin.)

Role differentiation seems to be more easily changed and more readily accepted than in the general American culture. There is a lessening of firm identification toward any one role taken, although the biological family roles are given prominence over work roles. For example, the role of motherhood is given considerable emphasis and social support and approval. This is perhaps well illustrated by the increasing custom of childbirth taking place at home with or without a trained attendant. The members of the tribal family and often-times friends are present during the birth. The delivery takes place to the accompaniment of prayers, chanting, drumming, and so forth. At these ceremonial gatherings, just as at weddings and funerals, children of all ages may be present. The child is welcomed ceremoniously into the world. There is, as yet, no set ritual or organized ceremonies. (As a physician, I would note that the incidence of complications appears no higher than usual.) The ability of the mother to respond immediately to her new-born is noteworthily high.

Children are usually well cared for, calm, and healthy; however, child-rearing on the fringes of the Awakened Society can be grim. A lack of parental stability here leads to migratory habits which, combined with inexperienced young mothers, can lead to malnutrition and neglect.

Continuing individual commitment without legally-enforced contract sanctions is the basis of the tribal family group. Perhaps this will change as greater numbers of families have children, and as the family members now in their twenties mature into the fourth and fifth decades of life. Nevertheless, the philosophical emphasis and personal commitment at this time are on renewal and reaffirmation through a continued voluntary association, rather than a marital contractual relationship.[4] On one hand, open emphasis on the necessity for the individual to continually reaffirm the relationship is a source of creativity, permitting the recognition and the resolution of latent problems.[5] On the other hand, this situation is fertile ground for lost opportunities and a source of instability and breakup of relationships.

I have sought out Awakened persons engaged in this type of community over the past several decades, some now in their fifties and sixties. These persons are generally more alert, more aware of their world, and more receptive to the idea of change and regeneration of both the individual and the family group than the usual middle-class person. They uniformly appear younger by about ten years. This is not to say that the tribal family structure as discussed here is the entire source of this greater life and spontaneity. Probably the persons engaged in this, having survived repeated trials and defeats as well as successes, are unique people anyway.

In the Society of the Awakened, marriage is optional and undertaken, if at all, usually for the sake of the children. Even this child focus

---

[4] Certainly, legal marriage, and divorce, do occur in this society.

[5] Dr. Gerald Smith of San Mateo points out that the awakened person expects much more of a relationship than does the usual middle-class person. Hence, the traditional criticisms of a "trial marriage"—that it is too fragile or that it can't stand real conflict—do not apply. The reason? Basic to the life style of the awakened person is a kind of intensity and intimacy in relationship which makes for resiliency and "ability to respond" (responsibility) even in a relationship as traditionally insecure as trial marriage.

is changing because of the increasing disillusionment of the society with the values and goals of the materialistic, power- and security-oriented American society. Paternity and legally-enforced monetary support is felt less important than the presence of a warm, loving, and stable maternal relationship, and supportive, accepting friends.

Older persons ("older" must be defined as "being in their thirties and forties") are the principal leaders around which the majority of families organize. In some of the intentional families the presence of a patriarch or matriarch is the actual basis of the family, much like the traditional family clans that already exist throughout the country. These older persons frequently are persons of exceptional ability who have, in effect, organized unconventional families around their own personalities. Such persons are usually self-employed or professional; in a few instances they are recognized professional therapists whose patients have come to view them as informal, but nevertheless real, heads of extended family systems. The head of such a family thus forms a spontaneous clan system, replacing the loss of this ancient system resulting from increasing diffusion of life in highly mobile America. High geographic mobility is a characteristic of these family clans; systems that have lasted over five years, however, tend to have one stable center of residence around which the family organizes. Members of the family may live as far as a thousand miles away and still view themselves as family members.

More and more family groups are emphasizing economic self-sufficiency through the work of family members. Again, a wide variety of patterns can be seen, having in common a pooling of the results of labor for the benefit of the family. In the simplest form, this may be an association of young people living in a common apartment on a very simple diet. Under these circumstances, one or two out of a group of a dozen work, sometimes at conventional jobs, sometimes in less highly organized jobs in the post office. Their money or "bread" will be used to buy the basic life necessities for the group. At a certain point, the working individual will give up his job and some other member will take over so that there is attained the goal of maximum leisure for self-fulfillment. Although there are many tirades against "hippies" as "social parasites," "welfare bums," and so forth, uncommonly do members of the Society of the Awakened receive welfare. When this does occur, it is principally among mothers of young children.

Tribal families range in size from half a dozen to perhaps fifty persons. A more definite roster cannot be given as there tend to be several dwelling places; it is difficult to tell an acknowledged family member from a non-family member who is a close and intimate acquaintance. Also, there is an overlapping of tribal families so that a given individual may be a member of several families. Another phenomenon is that a person or a couple may undertake to travel for a while, visiting from one family to the next. Under these circumstances, the tribal family membership undergoes a constant, although not rapid, turnover.

Summary

Abandoning automatic concurrence with traditional patterns of individual, mate, familial, and social relationships, an increasing number of white, middle-class young persons are building new social structures based on the re-evaluation through direct experience of customary values and behavior. This subculture puts a high value on experiencing the present (the Now Experience) in preference to the past or future. The Society of Awakening embodies as working life guides the traditional humanistic values of individual choice, reverence for life, pacifism, giving of self as well as material goods, respect for poverty joined to disrespect for material possessions, plus the customary emphasis on handcrafts, folk and popular music, and direct experience of nature. Unattached adolescents and adults make up the largest part of the society. Many are already disillusioned through childhood separations and have divorced themselves from traditional family demand, from goals of material rather than emotional satisfaction, and from other conditional gratifications.

Three values stand out: re-examination of socially-inculcated patterns through direct experience; a deep distrust of unverified authority; and joy in living in the present.

The tribal families are seeking a Camelot, a brotherhood and sisterhood of sharing, loving, and growing. Total sharing of body, spirit, and possessions is sought, though seldom achieved.

The significance of these families is their counter-thrust to the prevailing American materialistic society and its increasing view of the human being as only a unit in the social machine. Love and open life are gently opposed by the Awakened to abstract intellectual controls, computers, machinery, and death.

American advertising's exploitation of eroticism in the service of increased consumption has reduced the genital potency of the American male, and the loving warmth of the American woman. The Awakening culture re-establishes general sensual awareness, not solely genital intercourse, as the grounds for being, for existing, for being fully alive.

In an increasingly dissolving formal society, we can expect more such informal group living arrangements. The pattern developing is this: only a small minority of persons will be attracted to group living; the majority will have stable family ties and be socially conditioned to be conventional and unadventuresome. The few social explorers will predominantly be alienated, above-average single persons of various ages. If young, they will gravitate to the "Ellis Islands" of the awakening subculture, the growing "hippy" centers in every major city. Here they will find like-minded souls, and take up loosely-affiliated group living. Most will return to their former lives after a few weeks or months and resume more or less conventional life patterns. A minority will become established and enter more stable dyadic or group relationships.

A few older persons made single for various reasons will also enter the awakened culture. Some will have had a vision of a wholer, fuller life, free of the conventional role barriers to emotional contact existing in most American middle-class families. These will form other "intentional" communities comprised of like-minded persons seeking to share.

Conclusion

The tribal family is a natural experiment, under violently changing life conditions. The Society of Awakening is an evolutionary attempt to fit social responsibility to essential human needs; the general American society would do well to support rather than suppress this subculture.

VICTOR KASSEL

12

Polygyny after Sixty *

During the past fifteen years in the private practice of geriatrics, I have noticed a change in the attitude of many aged patients. Earlier in my career, these people felt a greater personal responsibility for working out the solutions to their own problems. Although they recognized the need for guidance to help effect a solution, they tended to assume a more active role in solving these problems. The aged have changed. Now, they have become passive, except to challenge everybody else to improve their lot. Their disabilities have become status symbols, a means whereby they can obtain attention and control their families. Years ago, these people considered old age a disadvantage and preferred that the nation ignore their chronological age. Now the aged are asking for special advantages because they are elderly. The emphasis has changed from what the aged can do to help themselves to what America can do to help the aged. Today, the needs of the aged are a major concern of our nation.

In considering these needs it is best to categorize them into three main groups: medical-surgical, psychiatric-psychological, and social. The aged concentrate mostly on their medical-surgical and psychiatric-psychological needs. But in the private practice of geriatrics, the greatest frustrations arise when trying to fill their social necessities. This would include needs caused by the death of a spouse, economic limitations due to inflation, decline of prestige, loss of status, compulsory retirement from business, and, most of all, inability to find fully satisfying activities. Unlike the treatment directed against a medical illness, where the physician participates actively in helping the patient, the acceptance or modification of the social problems must be done by the patient. More

* Reprinted from *Geriatrics*, vol. 21 (April 1966). Copyright 1966 by Lancet Publications, Inc.

and more the aged have become unwilling to try to change their lot. Rather, they look to society to modify itself to suit their needs. They seek to regain the way they lived in earlier adulthood. They would resurrect their dead spouses; they would undo the industrial advances of today. Many seem to say: "You've done this to me, now fix it!" I even have had patients blame me because they've lived so long; now they claim it is my responsibility to make them happy.

What can be done about it? The aged are with us and, in increasing numbers, they shall continue to be with us. If the aged find it so difficult to change, perhaps society might change so that the aged may be reintegrated and live comfortably.

During the past two hundred years, we have seen a gradual change in political, economic, and social philosophy in this country. Of the unfilled social needs of the aged which the social scientists have identified, there is a set which a certain change in our present social philosophy or ethic might fill. Many might consider this change radical, but it is a return to a practice which at one time was considered proper in the Judeo-Christian ethic. I mean a change to polygyny—a limited polygyny —polygyny after sixty.

Advantages Offered by Polygyny after Sixty

Greater ratio of older women to older men. With the American concept of equal rights and opportunities, not only all older men but also all older women would have the chance to marry or remarry following the death of a spouse. The average wife can expect to outlive her husband five to fifteen years so that, after the age of sixty, the women out-number the men. Thus, the need for polygyny is obvious: there just are not enough men. Therefore, any man over age sixty could marry two, three, four, or five women over sixty. Were the situation reversed and the men out-numbered the women, then polyandry would be the answer. Thus, there is a chance that polygyny would offer to the excess women the opportunity to obtain a husband. The inability of many older widows to remarry because of the limited number of available men represents an unfilled need which polygyny could help to alleviate.

The family constellation. Besides the opportunity to remarry, polygyny offers to these women the opportunity to re-establish a meaningful family group. Sociologists have stressed the importance of the family in American life. Our urban living has limited the size of the modern family in contrast to the size of the rural family during the last century. And likewise, our homes are large enough only for the parents and children of the modern family. There just is not enough room in the average modern home for three generations. In addition, changing ideas about child-raising often bring conflict between parents and grand-parents. Consequently, except as baby-sitters, grandparents cannot play a meaningful role in the modern family circle. They are not intimates in the family constellation; they are outsiders. With polygyny, there would be a return to the married state for the many lonely widows, as well as a chance to establish a genuine, intrarelated family group composed of these married women and their spouse.

Diet. Studies have demonstrated that married couples subsist on a more adequate diet than do widows and widowers. The lonely women, who were once excellent cooks, have no one for whom to prepare a complete meal. There is no incentive to cook. Many men never could cook well so they, too, live on a limited, unbalanced diet. On the other hand, where there is a group of people living together as a family, eating in the company of one another, the story is different. Mealtime regains its social atmosphere; appetites return. Each wife can take her turn at cooking so that the task does not become too great, and menu-planning becomes a source of pride. This can lead only to better and more adequate meals.

Living conditions. Another cause for the inadequate diet of aged men and women, besides the loneliness described above, is their limited income. And limited income contributes to the inadequate living conditions found among many aged. The polygynous marriage offers the opportunity to pool funds so that there is enough money for all. The family can live more graciously.

Illness. Added to the opportunities to maintain good health, another advantage of polygyny relates to illness. Many aged persons would not need nursing home care if responsible people at home were available to nurse the infirm person. In addition, many aged are hospitalized because they live alone and are unable to obtain adequate home nursing care. Polygyny solves this difficulty, for the husband and wives would take turns nursing the sick. Also, the care does not become too great a burden for one person as so often happens in monogomous marriages; the responsibility is shared. Added to these advantages is the fact that the ill person remains within the familiar surroundings of his or her own home.

Housework. Many aged find it impossible to keep their homes in order because of the fatigue produced by the physical labor of housework. Two or more women in a polygynous marriage, working together to keep the house in order, lighten the burden for one another. They also have an opportunity to display their abilities as fine homemakers without overworking themselves. In addition, when one of the wives finds her physical infirmity activated, she need not strain herself. She can rest, knowing full well that the other wives will continue the homemaking until she is capable again.

Sex. Now we come to the most delicate and the most controversial aspect. Studies at various geriatric centers have disproved the misconception that older people are not interested in sexual activity. Marriage sanctions sexual activity, and the polygynous marriage enables the unmarried older woman to find a partner. Most widows refrain from sex because they lack this partner; society has taught women to remain chaste when not married.

To many people it is abhorrent to visualize grandparents or even parents past the childbearing stage enjoying the pleasures of sexual intercourse. Older women, recognizing this attitude, repress their sexual desires and develop psychological conflicts and consequent guilt. Studies have demonstrated, however, that most women have an increase in libido after the menopause simply because they lose the fear of pregnancy. A polygynous marriage enables them to express this desire, instead of remaining repressed through a continent widowhood.

As for the men, sexologists claim that the male is polygynous by nature. The development of impotency and decreased libido in older men need not represent a senile change. The existence of a climacteric in the male has never been positively established. It seems that most impotency in the aged male represents boredom and many times an unattractive, uninterested partner. With variety, greater interest is sparked and many men can come back to life sexually. Also, the problem of the frigid wife is eliminated; other partners are available. Polygynous marriage offers a solution to a number of sexual problems of the aged.

Grooming. Where you have many women competing for the attention of the lone male, both the women and the man would show an increased interest in better grooming. Many aged persons are uninterested in their appearance, change their undergarments infrequently, bathe inadequately, and seldom cleanse their external excretory organs. Polygyny offers to the woman someone for whom to compete. The man, on the other hand, is interested in being courted. Each person will do his or her best to upgrade appearances, each will be alert to the advantages gained by the competitor, and each will learn the tricks of becoming more attractive. The end result must be finer-appearing older citizens.

It can be argued that the jealousy aroused as the result of the competition would be carried to an extreme by the women and would disrupt the quiet, peaceful home. This may occur. But when there is a choice between uninterested, dowdy, foul-smelling hags, and alert, interested, smartly dressed ladies, the selection is obvious. Troubles might arise, but what marriage—monogomous or polygynous—is without troubles? The strained competition between the women does represent an obvious disadvantage of this married state, but the advantages compensate for this one difficulty.

Depression and loneliness. In the practice of geriatrics, one of the major psychiatric problems encountered is depression. As mentioned above, the aged no longer find themselves members of a family. The result is loneliness and a feeling of uselessness on the part of the aged parent. Depression results from this loneliness and uselessness. These people always ask, "What is the point of my existence?" There is no answer that seems to satisfy them; they find no reason to continue living. In our youth-centered, family-oriented society, the aged find their own youth gone and their family grown. Depression results. Their children may try to make work for them in order to re-establish the parents' importance and feeling of being needed, but the contrivance is obvious. The sham only produces a deeper depression.

Although the polygynous family group is not the same as the youthful, monogamous family, at least it is the closest thing to it. In contrast to the monogamous marriage, polygyny frees a larger percentage of older women from the loneliness and depression of widowhood.

Since this is polygyny after the age of sixty, the married partners will be close in age, with a greater likelihood of similar interests. This would spur a more intimate socialization between members of the family so that they could attend community activities and programs together. When living alone, the aged are reluctant to participate in activities outside their home. When living with others, however, interests are more likely to become contagious. The married partners can engage in activities as a family. It is knowing that one is a member of a distinct group that produces a feeling of belonging, with a consequent reason to live.

In addition, polygyny enables a number of people to live together intimately. Each one has lived his unique life, and each one enters the marriage with a different set of experiences. There is then the chance for each member of the marriage to grow further by his close contact with the other members of the family. Each can learn from the experiences of the others, and in that way deepen his insight into life. Living alone seldom offers this opportunity.

Thus, a polygynous marriage in old age is capable of dispelling depression and loneliness, as well as enabling the participant to grow in depth.

Health insurance. The final advantage of a polygynous marriage in the later years has to do with health insurance. Recent years have seen the growth of group health insurance. Membership in it offers advantages over individual policies. For example, Utah Blue Cross and Blue Shield is less expensive and more inclusive when the insuree is part of a group plan. Older persons who, upon retirement, elect to continue their health insurance find their premiums more expensive, and they are excluded from psychiatric benefits. There is no reason why group insurance should not consider the polygynous family within its coverage and charge less expensive premiums.

Summary

Polygyny after sixty is offered for consideration as a solution to a number of the social problems of the aged. This modification of marriage is not unique in the history of our culture. At one time it was a socially acceptable way of life. Today, too many aged persons find it impossible to adjust to the social changes that occur in their senescence. Less and less are they able to establish a meaningful role for themselves in American society, and much unhappiness has been the result. They have become less aggressive and more passive while waiting for solutions to be effected for them, and they seem contented in allowing the nation to grant them special privileges merely because they are elderly. Therefore, it would seem that society should attempt to find solutions to these problems. Polygyny after sixty could insure the elimination of a certain set of the aged's social problems, even though it meant a total change in certain aspects of the structure of marriage. The writer fully recognizes that the introduction of polygyny after sixty entails many complications, but he feels certain that the advantages gained for the aged would more than compensate for the trouble necessary to work through these difficulties. Thus, if the aged refuse to solve these problems for themselves, then, rather than allow the aged to continue in their miserable, unhappy state, society must change.

13

The Intimate Network of Families
as a New Structure

As dramatic as forecasts of doom for the American family may be, they are, fortunately, highly premature. Ever since the behavioral sciences first became interested in the relationships between early experience, family structure, and subsequent personality development, the family (and, in particular, parents) has become the scapegoat of rising rates of delinquency, mental illness, divorce, educational problems, and other social ills too numerous to mention. Compelling as the relationship between such problems and developments within the family may be (and, this relationship is not at all clear beyond the fact that most people who develop problems have come from families), such fearful consequences of continuing family patterns will no more effect changes in family life than the fear of cancer has changed cigarette smoking patterns over a large segment of the population. (The relationship between cigarette smoking and lung cancer seems much more clearcut than the consequences of conducting one's family life in a particular way.)

The fearful consequences of continuing family structures as they exist now are much too irregular and too distant either to deter potential parents or to alter their patterns for arranging their ways of life. As the findings of Blood and Wolfe [1] have indicated, people find the alternative of not having children empty and meaningless. It is the family experience, in and of itself, rather than any social consequence, which compels people to enter family life. Changes in family structure will occur, therefore, as a result of changes in the quality of the family experience, with small regard for the social effects they might produce.

[1] R. O. Blood, Jr., and D. M. Wolfe, *Husbands and Wives* (New York, The Free Press, 1960).

In this respect, the following statement found in the report of the Midcentury White House Conference on Children and Youth would have meaning only for professionals: "There are, however, some changes in American life that suggest that independence and self-reliance are somewhat less needed than formerly, and that the ability to value other people, to join in collective activities, and to stay put, may be among the especially highly regarded virtues of the future." [2]

In order to characterize the contemporary American family experience, it is tempting to paraphrase the oft-quoted lines of T. S. Eliot referring to the world ending with a whimper rather than a bang. For the quality of American family life is less in danger of a portentous fate than it is of becoming increasingly less variegated and less compelling for family members—that is to say, more boring. People turn to family life because the alternative may be even more appalling; due, however, to concepts prevailing in a significant spectrum of the American scene, they often settle for a family life—perhaps encompassing twenty-five to thirty of their adult years—which is often disappointingly limited in what it actually offers. Perhaps more than any other aspect of their lives, people accept the limitations of family living as inevitable; in no other phase of their lives are people apt to show as little creativity or as much acceptance of the *status quo* as the only possibility open to them.

Without attempting to paint family life in idyllic tones, certain trends in contemporary families can be specified as tending to place unnecessary burdens upon the family and as contributing, in a major fashion, to its emerging monochromatic features. The increasing isolation and independence of the conjugal family has resulted in an impoverished experience, thus placing an almost impossible burden on the family members by forcing them to carry out without aid tasks not easily accomplished in an insular fashion. As a way out of the dilemma, the development of relationships *between* families will be proposed.

The Independent American Family

To speak of *the* American family is to engage in a fiction since there are a great variety of familial forms and structures. Nevertheless, those

[2] Helen L. Witmer and Ruth Kotinsky, *Personality in the Making* (New York, Harper & Row, 1952), p. 200.

families considered part of the upwardly-mobile middle class [3] would appear to represent the type of family most people have in mind when they generalize about the American family. Scholars have engaged in some debate concerning the relative isolation of such families. Parsons [4] based his analysis of the family system on its growing separation from the extended family. Others have disagreed as to the extent to which this has occurred. As Goode [5] points out, contact is generally maintained with a wide range of relatives and it is rare for a nuclear family to be completely isolated from the family network.

Sussman and Burchinal [6] have gleaned the most data for the rejection of the concept of the isolated nuclear family and point out that considerable interchange of help takes place between elements of the extended family. However, Dager [7] has countered that this takes place in the context of increasing mobility which has become both broad and frequent. Under these circumstances, while contact with the extended family may be maintained, and help in a crisis extended, the contacts are of such an attenuated nature that they cannot play a vital role in the formation of identification, influence, and transfer of value systems.

A compelling description of such families is made by Seeley, Sim, and Loosley in their examination of the suburban community, Crestwood Heights.[8] What is most characteristic of the upper middle class families they portray is their geographic and social isolation from the extended family, despite the fact that contact may be made from time to time. The ideal for these families is that of separateness—both in terms of their physical habitation and the kinds of influence they encourage or sanction for their children. For such families, a man's home is indeed his castle. The value of the separate dwelling is so high that even an apart-

[3] Ruth S. Cavan, "Subcultural Variations and Mobility," in H. T. Christensen, *Handbook of Marriage and the Family* (Chicago, Rand McNally, 1964), pp. 535–581.

[4] T. Parsons and R. F. Bales, *Family, Socialization and Interaction Process* (Glencoe, Ill., The Free Press, 1955).

[5] W. J. Goode, *The Family* (Englewood Cliffs, N.J., Prentice-Hall, 1964).

[6] M. B. Sussman and L. G. Burchinal, "Kin Family Network: Unheralded Structure in Current Conceptualizations of Family Functioning," *Marriage and Family Living*, vol. 24 (1962), pp. 231–240.

[7] E. Z. Dager, "Socialization and Personality Development in the Child," in H. T. Christensen, *Handbook of Marriage and the Family* (Chicago, Rand McNally, 1964), pp. 740–781.

[8] J. R. Seeley, R. A. Sim and E. W. Loosley, *Crestwood Heights* (New York, Basic Books, 1956).

ment, separated though it may be from relatives, is considered inadequate for the optimum development of family life, as it does not provide an adequate distance from other families. It is as if a very real moat, consisting of the private property line, must surround the home. Mutual agreement between families concerning the appropriateness of intrusion into this private domain provides as adequate a barrier as the moat provided in more hostile times. The equivalent of the drawbridge is provided through the formal entry which is opened at the discretion of the family when acceptable approach motions are expressed by outsiders.

Implicit in such an arrangement are views concerning the conditions permitting the optimum development of a family. Independence is seen as being extremely important; autonomy is generally both an implicit and explicit goal. An unwitting consequence is a high degree of emotional interaction concentrated upon a few individuals, thus placing a continual strain upon the family experience. Parents in such families are highly goal-oriented, and the goal is defined as the production of appropriate character and personality. Anxiety over this goal is constant, coloring the experience of family life to a considerable degree.

In isolated families, parents loom as the *only* significant factor affecting the children; any interference impinging upon the intimate family is seen as a potential threat. It is as if these parents have set themselves up as expert child-rearers, and any difficulty with their children is seen as a direct reflection of their capacity in this area. When meeting quandaries (as would seem to be inevitable), they can rely only upon their own views of child-rearing. Faced with the dilemma—concern for the child versus concern for loss of face as to their skill as child-rearers—parents in these families have little choice but to become more rigid and insistent about their practices, thereby adding to the monotonous quality of the experience they are undergoing.

Parents, as adults, have needs which are separated and differentiated from the world of children. Where the family is independent and isolated, there are relatively few resources enabling the parents to attend to those needs which require separation from the children. Such needs must either be negated, or else fulfilled in competition with the needs of the offspring. Under such circumstances, guilty frustration tends to become maximized and straightforward satisfaction is rarely attained.

The richness of the family experience for the parents can partially be seen in Parsons' [9] terms relating it to the reliving of one's own child-

---

[9] T. Parsons and R. F. Bales, *op. cit.*

hood through participation in the lives of one's children. It is, therefore, the needs of the parents which are ultimately served by their own devotion and service to their children; by sharing in their offspring's lives, parents can serve a part of themselves never completely dead, but so often dormant: their own child-self. In addition, parents require the sense of importance given them when the children acknowledge the central role they play in their lives by reflecting back to them the introjection of parental values. Thus, influence, freely and openly acknowledged, is an important ingredient in the family experience.

For the children, an important part of the family experience is the sense of connectedness and separation which they constantly require as their needs shift between support and love, and the requirement to experience themselves as separate individuals. Consequently, the family experience for the child is, of necessity, highly ambivalent, more characterized by change than by fixed and settled characteristics. In addition, the child's rich experience is also related to other humans with whom he comes in close contact. He is, thus, given an opportunity to explore the variety of roles and characteristics that adults exhibit.

When the family is isolated, many of these aspects of the family experience can only be considered impoverished. The goal-oriented needs of the parents rob them of the ability to share and to experience their children's childhood; what will happen becomes more important than what is going on. In turn, because there are so few buffers between parents and children, the child's conflicting needs for support and for individuality are threatened. Since there is no one other than the parents for the child to turn to, he is unable to experience a richer variety of adult contact than the parents, themselves, can provide. His world, as a result, is smaller and less varied than might otherwise be the case.

Although parents may achieve their goals in these isolated families, becoming in fact the sole source of influence in the development of children, the effect of this influence is often substantially different from the effect intended. Elimination of the extended family as an effective source of values creates a vacuum not necessarily filled by the increased influence of the parents. Instead, the family merely becomes a single point of influence among a host of values to which the children are subjected. When the mother and father become the only effective models which the children can emulate, a multitude of other models appear to fill this void. Thus, we can see such social agencies as the schools taking over a greater portion of the role of value determiner. At the same time, it can be seen that the adolescent subculture, with its particular values and styles of life, has flourished to the degree that the family has become more isolated. The result is that the children turn away from the family for significant sources of influence (particularly because this turns out to be a grey, dull prospect for them). The immediate consequence, in terms of the family experience, is a heightened disappointment; tension develops over the adoption of values not family-sanctioned, and interest in what the adolescent children are doing and thinking (the shift between freedom and disinterest being a subtle but significant one) is lessened.

Raising a family inevitably involves difficulty, whether it be illness, financial stress, or emotional and behavioral problems. Given the limited room to maneuver that isolated families possess, these difficulties can present a greater strain than might be necessary. Only two alternatives are available: to become more self-reliant, or to reach out for professional help. Where the difficulty is partially a consequence of the parents' own behavioral patterns, self-reliance can become a liability, as the parents intensify behavior which was a major contribution to the problem. While reaching out for professional help can be of substantial aid in terms of the difficulties that are presented, it tends to enhance a quality isolated families frequently possess: a tendency to psychologize their family life.

The parents in these families often adopt (with their own unique interpretations) the personality theories of the professionals, perceiving much of their family experience less in terms of the immediate satisfactions available to them and more in terms of the personality effects they are producing. Their appreciation of the family experience is thus limited due to their concern for the "family products" they are turning out. They also become subject to the guilt such professional theories tend to generate, unaware that there are currents of fads and fashion within these theories, as Bronfenbrenner has pointed out.[10]

As we have said, the fact that there are rarely any buffers between parents and child makes the child's problems of connectedness and separation more highly charged than they might be. Such children are frequently placed in the position of either capitulating to their parents completely or of totally turning away from them. Lack of intimacy with

[10] U. Bronfenbrenner, "Socialization and Social Class through Time and Space," in Eleanor E. Maccoby, R. M. Newcomb and E. H. Hartley, Readings in Social Psychology (New York, Holt, Rinehart & Winston, 1958), pp. 400–425.

adults outside the immediate family circle also points up the closed experience an isolated family can become once the child is old enough to widen his circle beyond this immediate family. In an extended family situation there is often an excitement to the coming and going of family intimates; these dealings with parts of the intimate network can be rich without being as charged as the dealings with the parents inevitably are. A wealth of family rituals often arise around the comings and goings of these significant others; such rituals are not only interesting and enriching in their own right, but also permit a vast amount of emotional investment to be made with minimal storminess. In isolated families, with their emphasis upon the democratic structure of the intimate circle, such ritual is often conspicuous by its absence and there is relatively little differentiation made over the comings and goings of significant people. How this adds to the impoverishment of the family experience can only be left to the imagination.

The movement toward the isolated family may well be incompatible with a richer investment in family experience. It places enormous burdens upon the parents who must assume an expertise in the art of child-rearing which is not realistic for anyone. (Witness the relatively poor success members of the helping professions have as parents.) Under such an arrangement, parents are forced to become total parents, relinquishing a considerable portion of their own needs that lie outside the parents' role to such an extent that they experience disinterest and withdrawal. The children, deprived of intimacy with other adults, are subject to an impoverishment of experience and a lack of family ritual and ceremony, which diminishes the significant memories of family life they can carry with them into their own parenthood.

The Relationship between Families

As indicated, my concern is less with improving that abstract concept, society, than in enhancing the possibilities of rich, creative, fulfilling, and satisfying family experiences for the family members. The bulk of the argument, up to this point, has suggested that the family in isolation from others finds such rich experiences more difficult to attain. The alternative structure which is being proposed is the development of particular kinds of relationships and arrangements *between families*, i.e., intimate networks.

Under the circumstances previously described, the isolated family functions as a team when coming into contact with anyone outside the family circle. As described by Motz,[11] the family behaves much as if they had read Goffman's description of "front stage" and "back stage" performances carried out by teams that must deal with an audience or public.[12] All members of the family collaborate to maintain a particular appearance before others which is substantially different from that which they permit themselves when not in the presence of strangers. Any substantial experience with families in the presence of other families reveals how early the children learn to collaborate in this particular charade. A reordering of this type of family custom would be necessary for any enduring relationship between families to develop.

In view of the increasing mobility of the American family and the relatively low likelihood that the extended family could be revived as a significant part of the family experience, the compelling alternative involves the development of intimacy *between* several families. This arrangement has been called an *intimate network*, and specifies certain characteristics if the family experience is going to be affected in significant ways. Briefly defined, an intimate network of families could be described as a circle of three or four families who meet together regularly and frequently, share in reciprocal fashion any of their intimate secrets, offer one another a variety of services and do not hesitate to influence one another in terms of values and attitudes. Behind this definition is a picture of a brawling, noisy, often chaotic convocation which develops its own set of customs for the purpose of coming together in terms of rich experiences rather than merely being "correct" and, in the process, achieves movement in terms of its own views of its arrangements and ways of operating. Such an intimate family network would be neither stagnant nor polite but would involve an extension of the boundaries of the intimate family. In order to specify how this might come about, a closer look at the specifications of the intimate network is in order:

1. *A circle of families.* Once a set of parents have joined themselves to a group of families, they have acknowledged certain limitations of the isolated family. There is only a minimal vision of the potentialities of

[11] Annabelle B. Motz, "The Family as a Company of Players," *Trans-action*, vol. 2, no. 3 (1965), pp. 27–30.

[12] E. Goffman, *The Presentation of Self in Everyday Life* (Garden City, N.Y., Doubleday, 1959).

family life available to them because their experience with families outside their own childhood is nonexistent. Their own expertise as childrearers (particularly with their own children) is no longer pushed as a supreme illusion; the difficulty of the task is accepted and the need for continuous help, insight, and an occasional shakeup from outside their immediate family circle is accepted. They fact the possibility that the needs of various family members, including themselves, cannot be met without services being extended from outside the small circle of the immediate family. They realize that these services, when coming from community agencies rather than intimates, lack the meaning and warmth that could be a necessary part of the richer family experience.

The number of families to be accommodated within an intimate network should be sufficient to provide a variety of viewpoints and services, and a richness of close contact without blocking the sharing which would be a necessary feature of this arrangement. Two families would not be adequate to deal with many of the problems that would inevitably arise and would not provide enough variety. Depending upon the size of the families, judgment would similarly suggest that a group much beyond four would be difficult to manage. However, there is nothing inherent in such a number and experience could well alter this judgment.

2. *Regular and frequent meetings.* In order for intimacy and sharing to be attained and maintained, frequency of contact is required. Intimacy is a fragile quality and requires both frequency and regularity, particularly in the formative phases. When coming together is an infrequent occurrence, families will either be on their best behavior, or will reserve such consultations solely for major crises. It is one of the goals of the intimate network to explore not only the large, obvious issues of family living, but also, the mundane, day-to-day features which probably color family life more meaningfully than those aspects parents are likely to believe "important." Families that come together for the purpose of being honest with one another will obviously meet painful situations, the avoidance of which will be inevitable if there are clear escape routes through irregularity of contact. Knowledge of the other families, and the courage to be honest with one another, are expected to result from frequent and regular meetings.

3. *Reciprocal sharing.* While there are always limitations to what is shared, families in the intimate network would have to develop the freedom to permit the other families to peer behind the scenes. If help is to be sought and given, there must be an openness about what is needed.

Under such an arrangement, secrecy becomes as much a self-delusion as an attempt to confuse others about the reality that exists within the family. Therefore, such families must voluntarily be able to be open as to what is occurring, and as to the feelings and relationships that exist between all members, revealing to the others the details of how they live together. The retention of family secrets requires unwritten contracts within the family to be mutually protective at the cost of honesty; in order to maintain such collusion, a variety of subterranean agreements are required which can only be maintained at considerable cost.

Within the intimate network, the emphasis would, of necessity, have to be upon reciprocity. The burden is not upon a particular family to show themselves while the others withhold important aspects of their lives, nor upon one group of people to reveal themselves before a group of voyeurs, but rather, upon the circle itself to develop a freedom for all members to show themselves in a variety of ways and, as time goes on, with less and less reluctance. Should role patterns between families develop in an exclusively hierarchical order, a truly intimate network could not be established.

4. *Exchange of services.* A classic fairy story concerns a person offered three magic wishes, the clues these choices give to his values and the consequences they have for his life. In much the same fashion, a family faced with a possible exchange of services with other families is faced with an array of possibilities; the requests that are made will be a function of their version of the possibilities inherent in family living. Therefore, the types of requests made between the families within the intimate network will be important expressions of their versions of family life, and should change as these families engage in their mutual exploration of such potentialities. Actual help for crises would be one expected exchange of services. But on a less dramatic level one can envision the development of an interfamily consultation service in which various members of each family are called upon to aid in negotiations which are constantly required within families from time to time. It is entirely conceivable that the requests for services will move into more unexpected areas as the families become more creative about their arrangements for family living.

Implicit in the kinds of services that are created within the family network are versions of what is possible and what is available if creativity is applied toward family living. Accepting what is possible within the isolated family demonstrates a poverty of conceptualization about the conduct of one's life and an acceptance of what is given. What can be accomplished within an isolated family arrangement is extremely limited and the resources of any given family diminish the kinds of satisfactions that can be extended to the various members of the family. Therefore, the system of services that are developed within a network will be an important aspect of the creativity which is being applied to the circumstances of family living.

5. *The extension of values.* As the network becomes more intimate, that is, as members become increasingly more free to deal with one another in a spontaneous manner, there would be less and less reluctance to express whatever comes to mind toward members of other families. Ultimately, such a development would involve the attempt to influence the other families in terms of the values and attitudes they hold close. To the degree that there are differences between the families, such an interchange would not necessarily mean the adoption of one or another of these value systems, but rather, a tug of war between the varying world views. Out of this type of struggle it is conceivable that *an intimate network could develop new systems of attitudes and values that did not exist before in any of the member families.* Such a development would be dependent upon the method that the family networks developed to resolve deadlocks that arise between the members. The possibilities of values and attitudes based upon broader explorations than is generally the case gives rise to the possibility that richer and more realistic systems can be developed than is possible under the prevailing system of isolated families.

The Development of the Intimate Network

The concept of the intimate network of families arose from the development of the family workshop.[13] This technique of working with families represents a realistic means of developing such networks within the conceivable future. While true family networks have yet to be developed, the problems of developing relationships between families have received some initial exploration.

[13] F. H. Stoller and Ann Dreyfuss, "The Family Workshop: A Format for Enhancing Family Experience," mimeograph, 1967; and F. H. Stoller, "The New Groups," *Psychology Today* (1967).

The family workshop consists of three or four families meeting for a weekend for the purpose of exploring their operations and developing a more creative approach toward the arrangements within families. Although such workshops are therapeutic, they are not conceived as being therapy; rather, they are designed as growth experiences for families which, though they may have difficulties, are not necessarily "problem" families. The presence of many families is an essential feature of such workshops in that they provide a broader base for examining the nature of family life than a single family by themselves. The possibilities of exchanging functions within the workshop itself offers a broad base for discovery; families often even exchange members in order to work through complicated deadlocks.

Another inherent feature of such workshops is the development of openness when more than one family is present. Experience with the workshop indicates that sharing between families presents initial difficulties which take little time to alter when appropriate attitudes are present. It is not the *development* of intimacy which presents the major problem for the family network, but rather, the *retention* of intimacy within a culture in which the prevailing values and forms of family life are markedly different. Despite such difficulties, a number of families have maintained their relationships over time in such fashion as to constitute a partial development of the intimate network. Such families have utilized periodic meetings for the exploration of problems, have exchanged services such as providing freedom for the parents to take vacations from the children, and have served in a limited capacity as consultants for one another.

Some requirements for the full development of the intimate network have become clarified. One of the most important features is physical proximity—most likely the network has the most potential within the neighborhood structure. The regularity of meetings is another important feature, and in connection with this, some assistance from professionals would be of considerable help, particularly in the early phases when such an arrangement would be contrary to the force of social pressures surrounding the network which might not support its goals. The availability of professional consultation and the development of a sense of how to reach for such help without becoming dependent upon it is an important function of the network.

At the present time, a number of community agencies with an abiding interest in the "well" family have expressed interest in exploring the format of the intimate network. The plan would be to initiate the families with a number of family workshops and then to provide the networks with support in terms of places to meet, resources from the professional staff, and encouragement and interest in their ongoing development. At best, such a plan can only represent a necessary phase in the initial development of networks. Ultimately, networks would require a viable life of their own, independent of professionals, except for their interested support. In the final analysis, major values in the social system at large would require revision.

Privacy as a Value

The questions raised by the introduction of such a structure as the intimate network into the American family system center very closely on the requirements families have for privacy. Intrusions into the maintenance of privacy are increasingly seen as violations of the individual's integrity. Considerable emotional force can be generated when observing the growing trend toward invasion of privacy through a rapidly developing technological and organizational sophistication. Electronic eavesdropping and the growing investigative techniques of governmental and private agencies represent the involuntary invasion of privacy and only succeed in contributing toward a growing sense of helplessness in the individual. It should be clear that in developing the concept of the intimate network, it is not the unwilling surrender of the right to privacy that is at issue, but rather the voluntary movement back and forth between open sharing and self-contained areas of living.

As indicated earlier, privacy for families is often seen as a need, a requirement for the development of adequate personalities. Such thinking creeps into the very design of our structures around which we organize our lives, as the writings of such architects as Chermayeff and Alexander suggest.[14] However, a look at family life from the viewpoint of a social historian such as Ariès [15] indicates that homes were not formerly designed for separation but rather for connection. From Ariès' description, one surmises, for example, that the medieval home

---

[14] S. Chermayeff and C. Alexander, *Community and Privacy* (Garden City, N.Y., Doubleday, 1963).
[15] P. Ariès, *Centuries of Childhood* (New York, Random House, 1962).

was designed to let all segments of the family (including servants) inter-
mingle in all their functions and that honored visitors were taken into
intimate aspects of the family circle. At question here is not whether one
arrangement is necessarily better than the other, but that such organizations for family living represent values on a continuum rather than
absolute requirements.

A false dichotomy can be made between privacy and non-privacy,
between the communal arrangement and the isolated family. Both are,
of course, possibilities, with their liabilities and assets. Under discussion
here, however, is a different arrangement in which families have
consistent alternatives before them: to share or to hold to themselves.
To have never known privacy is, of course, to be robbed of the experience of separateness. However, to have never known the experience of
openness and sharing is to be denied the possibilities of interchange with
others. Exclusive adherence to either one of these polarities can only be
impoverishing; the individual is faced not with a choice but with a
limitation. The intimate family network, therefore, stands for a diversity
of experience, a moving between privacy and sharing rather than the
exclusive reliance upon one or the other.

The degree to which the coming together of families is facilitated or
hindered is a function of the kinds of arrangements that are made available. In this sense, aspects of architecture and urban planning, which
tend to fixate the values of the society at large, should not be ignored by
those who see some point to influencing social change. Homes, for
example, which are designed for exclusive privacy and do not provide for
any territory which belongs to a group of families thus facilitate the
isolated family. Yet planners can and do think in alternate ways as
Mayer indicated when he designed a structure for a low-cost housing
community which he designated as "Everybody's Club" and which is
multifunctional.[16] Many architects, such as Chermayeff and Alexander,[17]
and city planners such as Jacobs,[18] are deeply concerned about the
consistently boring and deadly aspects their designs and organizations
are presenting to the urban dweller; they are now paying consistently
more attention to creating heightened variation and interest. Since there

[16] A. Mayer, *The Urgent Future* (New York, McGraw-Hill, 1967).

[17] S. Chermayeff and C. Alexander, *op. cit.*

[18] Jane Jacobs, *The Death and Life of Great American Cities* (New York, Knopf,
1961).

has been a parallel interest in the possibilities of a more highly variegated family life, it is possible that attention to organizations and arrangements within social institutions (and the physical arrangements that parallel them) could be a fruitful and exciting exploration.

Summary

The increasing mobility of the American family creates greater isolation from the extended family—which results in a family experience that is not as rich, fulfilling, or creative as is possible. Limiting rather than enhancing, the isolated family tends to become more rigid and impoverished in terms of the influence, satisfaction, and ritual generated. An alternative structure is seen in the *intimate network of families*, in which three or four families come together on a regular basis to explore their living arrangements, to exchange intimacies, to provide services for one another, and to develop new and more realistic, and more exciting, systems of values and attitudes. Initial explorations or relationships between families have already been explored in family workshops and present a feasible base for introducing such a structure into American society.

CARL LEVETT

14

A Parental Presence
in Future Family Models

One of the obvious and gnawing dilemmas of the contemporary
American family scene is the side-effects that accelerated individualization has had on parent-child relationships. The family structure,
steeped in the rural traditions of cohesive interdependence, is inexorably
being replaced by an urban family configuration whose members find
increasing resolution of personal need and development through extra-
familial involvements. Perhaps no one family member has been more
affected by this centrifugal process than the paternal figure. His search
for financial solvency and occupational success has become increasingly
intertwined with exercising his highly specialized skills in a rapidly
expanding automated society. An increasing share of his interpersonal
involvement occurs within that industrial complex as a member of an
alter-family of executives, associates, and secretaries.

The demands on the father's participation within a second family
have led to a "vacuum of presence" in those personal areas of family
living where he was formerly more fully involved. It is within the
father-child relationship that the impact of a father *in absentia* has been
keenly felt. The "old-fashioned" approach of father's hand being there
to guide and discipline the children no longer asserts itself as it once did.

When a breakdown in family integration which centers on a male
offspring occurs, it is current practice to cast the father in the role of
the villain and to attempt to reinvolve him in paternal responsibilities
that are tied to the traditional family model: "You don't spend enough
time with your son." Such admonitions have not provided a resolution
of the basic problem. Each generation of young men continues to
struggle desperately for a sense of self in the face of a diminishing
paternal presence. Each generation of fathers searches for new ration-

alizations to expiate the guilt that accures from so-called paternal neglect. With the family structure in transition, it is fruitless to look backward for solutions to emerging transformations. Yet, how can the family go forward? How can new approaches be applied to this changing model?

Future family configurations will need to form and meander freely rather than to be adjusted to a fixed and preconceived traditional formulation. If this concept can be accepted, then so can a changing family model whose paternal figure no longer serves the classical father-son child-rearing role. Under such circumstances, innovative and untried options for dealing effectively with the dynamic changes in family models become possible.

With paternal figures in diminishing supply, greater use will need to be made of supplementary masculine resources to close the father-son guidance gap. One direction a future model may take is to depart from the narrow belief that only the blood-kin father can provide the essentials of masculine identification for the male child. The trend toward specialization of skills and talents will make possible the emergence of a "third parent," a male figure educated, trained, and equipped to serve the socializing needs of male children. Substitutive forms of help from paternal figures (such as camp counselors, pediatricians, school psychologists, and scoutmasters) are being offered to young males in increasing degrees. Such efforts are essentially piecemeal and lace the continuity of the breadth-and-depth involvement of a third-parent relationship aimed at serving the whole child in terms of potentiality release, parental and family integration, peer participation, and development of sound personal values.

The evolution of a third-parent model is likely to begin in family establishments whose fathers function in a free-form manner. These men, highly respected and successful in their own fields of endeavor and heavily committed to extra-familial responsibilities, are people-oriented as well as performance-oriented; they retain a sincere concern and devotion for their children's welfare, but because of limitations of time and energy are unable to provide a personal and responsive flow of contactual experience with their sons.

An assessment of the specific ways a third parent might contribute to a changing family model leads to certain interesting projections. Such a venture could be initiated on a limited scale starting with a pilot program of selected families. Criteria for selection might include: age of parents, number of children, emotional stability of family members, degree of compatibility of the mother and father, and the desire of all family members to join in such a program. Both parents would need to relate and function in a venturesome spirit of discovery and mutual cooperation. In a broad sense, selection would include those family models that were well-functioning and whose basic goals and values were toward self-realization of all family members. The essential deprivation adversely affecting the self-actualizing family processes would involve the lack of presence of the real father in regard to full paternal involvement. The purpose of a third parent's presence would be to correct this deficiency and to help liberate and renew the self-realizing values within such family models.

A third-parent program could be organized with young males as early as the first grade, at an age level of six to seven. This should be an appropriate time inasmuch as it coincides with a youngster's introduction to a real world more demanding than he has previously known. It is a moment when he would strongly feel the need for paternal support and guidance as an addition to the earlier years of maternal child-rearing.

A third parent's activities would comprise a number of important areas of functioning. The first of these would concern the relationship the third parent would maintain with each boy on an individual basis. Certainly, this aspect of the program would be quite crucial with respect to establishing empathy, rapport, and a deepening sense of trust in the relationship. The implication is that the third parent would need to exercise considerable sensitivity and artfulness in cultivating a paternal presence that had more and more value and meaning for the child.

It is likely that the initial phase of a third-parent involvement would be experienced with awkwardness and some resistance by a youngster. The threat of excessive personal exposure in a somewhat strange and undefined relationship, if handled with skill, could be converted, in all likelihood, into a growing source of satisfaction for the child as the dimensions of the relationship became better known. Nevertheless, one could anticipate a continuing testing on the part of the child to establish the limits of the third parent's presence. It would hardly be conceivable that the youngster would not attempt at various times to split the authority of mother and third parent: "Mr. So-and-So said I could." The dynamics of the testing would follow the usual script of what occurs when the natural father is an actively involved member of the family. Each encounter, if viewed in the context of representing another opportunity for personal and family integration, could serve as an added contribution for growth and self-actualization.

Are there other repercussions that one might expect from a third parent presence? One can foresee the relationship between mother and father undergoing a process of restructuring with the inclusion of so important a figure as the third parent. Not only will the role of both parents be subject to revision but any changes that occur are likely to raise associative questions: To what extent will the father's underlying distress in "not being there" as a paternal figure be dissolved? Will he be freer to participate with the family in new ways once the father-son commitment is transferred to the third parent? What kinds of feelings and attitudes will emerge for the mother who can now turn to an alter-father for guidance and assistance in fulfilling her maternal obligations? Will the interposition of the third parent release both natural parents from child-rearing pressures to the extent that their marital relationship may benefit and become more companionable?

The third parent's involvement with other members of the family model could activate interpersonal processes of an equally complex and challenging nature. The mother's position would shift in that she would now have an active paternal figure to share in her son's guidance. One could foresee where this would tend to catalyze a mixture of emotions within her. A degree of confusion might arise in her effort to reconcile the responsibility and relative authority of two paternal figures. Only after considerable working through of numerous issues still unforeseen could she be expected to legitimize the realistic boundaries to be accorded the two father figures. One could also foresee that she could no longer maintain her parental authority without revealing her maternal child-rearing practices to the scrutiny of the third parent. If her intentions are to use the third parent's presence constructively, however, the new partnership could provide a furthering release of maternal resources within her. It is conceivable that such learning might spark a material improvement in her handling of the other children in the family.

It could be anticipated that the third parent's relationship with the natural father would be more superficial. The real father's presence would be based on the kinds and degrees of delegated support he gives the third parent in the latter's attempt to function jointly, freely, and effectively with both mother and son. The third parent will be dependent on the actual father's subordination of competitiveness, authoritarianism, and jealousy in favor of the larger purpose of serving his son's personal needs. Yet, if the natural father can organize himself constructively within the context of the helping program, it is likely that a meaningful form of dependence on the third parent could accrue for him as well. The third parent will be favored by the real father's latent desire to provide a truly committed paternal presence for his son. The tensions that might develop between the natural father and third parent are likely to dissolve commensurate with the benefits that are realized by all family members. If the natural father can perceive the long-term values of the third parent's presence on behalf of his son, he will also recognize the potential promise the experience may provide with regard to a deepening and real father-son relationship in later years.

Another area requiring an artful interpersonal approach would involve other siblings. What kinds of attitudes will they have regarding the presence of a third parent who serves the needs of only one brother? How will they express their true feelings? Will they attempt to justify their own need for a third parent by presenting new-found problems of their own making? Here, the third parent is again likely to encounter the multitude of reactions and responses so commonplace in most family models. One could expect the other children to look upon the third parent as an intruder and usurper of the natural father's rightful presence. The mother's attitude toward such responses will be critical, either serving to undercut or reinforce the loosely defined third parent's authority. It would not be surprising to find the subject-son using the third parent as a foil with sister or brother. Nevertheless, given the underlying and continuing support of both parents, most of the resistances and devices used to circumvent a realistic family living process should be subject to resolution by a well-functioning third parent.

An expanded family selection program would make it possible for a third parent to organize a unit of from twelve to fifteen boys, a vehicle for carrying out periodic group experiences on a variety of levels. During formative years activities could be centered on recreational and athletic pursuits under third-parent supervision. Field trips for educational purposes, fitted to the age level of the group, could also be used as a means of stretching and widening the experiential horizons of the youngsters. Visits to museums, to historical settings, to industrial, municipal, and agricultural plants, would comprise some of the possible excursions. As the boys matured, group experiences could be used as a means of serving more personal needs. With a third parent acting as leader, group experiences could offer the boys a means to relate and share personal difficulties and frustrations in their attempt to resolve mutually pressing problems, whether in the interpersonal and sexual areas, or in regard to establishing a set of values consistent with the self-realizing process.

Another area in which the third parent could offer a meaningful presence would be the school. In addition to being a liaison between the home and school, the third parent would carry a parental responsibility that would manifest itself in a deep interest and concern on behalf of the children served. As of now, school systems are accustomed to relating themselves almost exclusively to mothers in evaluating a child's school work and adjustment. Yet, there is reason to believe that as a paternal, male, figure the third parent would be positioned to add another dimension to child-school-family integration by establishing a dialogue with school personnel that could not be achieved with a family model which presented only a "faceless" father figure. Granted that the school authorities might first look upon the third parent's incursions with suspicion and misgivings, there is no doubt that, with the advent of mutual understanding, significant and productive long-term benefits could accrue. Third parent participation could offer a more holistic approach to child-school-home dynamics and provide school administrations with an updated and continuing appraisal of the youngster's progress in regard to effectiveness of teaching methods and procedures. In addition, it is likely that teachers and school officials would find the third parent, by virtue of professional training and experience, to be a valuable resource in the counter-point of school and third parent involvement.

The credentials and qualifications of a third parent should be viewed in the framework of a professional career. The background of education, training, and experience would need to be heavily weighted in the areas of education, psychology, and social work. Graduate work leading to a master's or doctorate degree would be a logical necessity. Third parent pioneers would be expected to have at least ten years of highly rated, paid, professional experience in order to bring an established and mature competence to the program. In looking ahead, there is the possibility that a community agency, a university, or a foundation may initiate such a pilot study. However, to be truly effective, the program will require a third parent's professional participation full time. In all likelihood, the emerging needs of future family models will be more disposed to free-lance third parents, who will function very much like private practitioners. Furthermore, affiliation with communal institutions might inhibit and dampen the experimental quality of work and tend to depersonalize the character of the third parent-family relatedness. Perhaps some of the initial third parents will be those educators who have administered summer camps for boys. The carry-over to a third-parent program would be a logical extension of their developing capacities and skills in this realm of work.

To be self-supporting, a third parent's practice would need to include two groups of boys, or a total of thirty youngsters. Such a workload would compare favorably with acceptable caseload practice. A fee of from seven hundred and fifty to one thousand dollars per child would provide an adequate income. The program could parallel a nine-month school year with the customary summer break.

Since the third parent program would be perceived as a project requiring continuity, terminating with high school graduation, only a settled and well-established professional is likely to have arrived at a point of occupational stability to insure such a continuing presence.

To establish and maintain an ethical and professional quality of practice, a third-parent program would require an interdisciplinary base. This would imply that a team, comprising a psychologist, psychiatrist, pediatrician, social worker, educator, and research social scientist, would act as a control in reviewing the work of the third parent. Periodic meetings with the professional staff would be held on a consulting and supervisory basis. Remuneration to the staff would be derived from the third parent's private practice fees. The research specialist would recommend procedures for ensuring that records and files were properly maintained for possible future publication of scientific findings.

Beyond serving the needs of the third parent, an interdisciplinary base of professionals would also provide an integrity to the program. Parents and school officials, as well as community members, are likely to feel reassured that professional supervision and control is an essential part of such a program.

What can one envisage if an attempt is made to peer beyond a third parent family model? A case may eventually be made for a fourth parent presence. The contemporary pressures for greater self-fulfillment and self-actualization also appear to be stirring the distaff side toward greater individualization and independence. No longer are many well-educated wives and mothers satisfied to linger passively in the kitchen with a world about them that piques their curiosity and arouses passionate hungers within them to experience. It is conceivable that a fourth parent, a feminine counterpart, could serve as an ancillary mother for young daughters deprived of an adequate maternal presence. Such an arrangement may be particularly appropriate in situations where the woman is highly successful in a career and restricted, therefore, in providing a satisfactory maternal presence.

Third and fourth parents could become valuable resources in serving the needs of children of those divorced, when the child's adaptability is adversely affected by the fracturing of the parental relationship. Since the court usually awards the mother custody of the children, a third parent presence would be useful in many such instances to fill the paternal void. Nevertheless, the availability of both third- and fourth-parent programs could provide a flexible approach to marital breakdown.

Although third- and fourth-parent programs are likely to progress within a private practice frame of reference, future family models will also be affected by what is done in the public sector. It is reasonable to expect that community agencies will be called upon to deliver increasing remedial and preventive services to plug the parental gap. Remedial help for children, in the form of guidance clinics, family counseling agencies, and residential treatment centers, has existed for many years. Such help, essentially therapeutic in nature, has been beneficial for a limited population in reducing the emotional and psychological damage resulting from an impoverished parental presence. The real hope for future family models will depend on the degree that children's emotional disorders can be prevented. Without making such progress, the demands for remedial treatment for children could become staggering.

Some strides in the area of prevention are being made in the public service domain. The "Big Brother" program, instituted by numerous family counseling agencies, is a movement which attempts to serve the needs of young, fatherless, boys. Drawing on interested and available men in the community, the agency attempts to provide a paternal presence for such youngsters by acting as an agent in bringing man and boy together in hope of establishing a meaningful and companionable relationship for each. "Head Start" and "Follow Through" are publicly sponsored school programs intended, as preventive measures, to overcome the deficiencies of early parental care. Under these programs, underprivileged children are given special attention to develop greater intellectual competence with the help of parental figures.

These are obvious signs of a growing official concern regarding proper parental presence. The trend toward greater community involvement in child-rearing activities is likely to affect the future roles of many public agencies. There is likely to be a more balanced mix between remedial and preventive services than is currently being rendered to family models. Many more preventive programs, comparable to "Big Brothers," will no doubt be inaugurated in which professionally trained caseworkers and psychologists will be involved.

In time, a separate publicly-sponsored professional group is likely to emerge out of numerous experimental projects, known perhaps as "Parental Counselors." Such individuals could serve, in a preventive way, the needs of the community as a whole, the courts, and the public school system.

Conclusion

It would appear that the contemporary family model is on the threshold of changes that require innovative reshaping. If the family model does not have to be anchored to traditional forms, new and improvised styles of child-rearing can possibly provide parental presence so often lacking for the child living in a fragmented family structure. With our present social milieu moving more toward the specialization of skills and talents, an acceptance of this condition can lead to a greater use of specialists to serve as alter-parents. Ultimately, a uniquely educated, trained, professional corps of alter-parents could help to overcome many parental deficiencies in future family models.

GEORGE S. ROSENBERG

15

Implications of New Models of the Family for the Aging Population

In 1965 the total population of the United States stood at 194.5 million, of which approximately 18.1 million people were 65 years and over. Thus, about 9.3 percent of the population had attained what is conventionally regarded as "old age." This proportion represents a high point in a trend in age structure which has been underway since at least the turn of the century. Between 1900 and 1950 the percentage of the total population 65 years and over had increased from 4.1 to 8.1. Whether, or to what degree, this trend can be expected to continue is problematical. Population projections are no less subject to error and the vagaries of events than other predictions concerning human behavior; and the estimate of the future state of affairs with respect to the aged therefore depends upon the kinds of assumptions regarding fertility and mortality which demographers are willing to make. It is possible to estimate from one census series that by the year 1985 the proportion of people 65 years and over will range between 9.1 and 10.4.[1] But Sheldon has given projections to the year 2000 which indicate that the aged population may lie anywhere between 8.9 and 12.9 percent of the total.[2] From such sources it would be fair to conclude that in the next decades we may expect a stabilization of the proportion of old people in our society, or perhaps some relatively small increase compared to that of the past sixty or seventy years. However, even on the assumption that there is no

---

[1] Computed from U.S. Bureau of the Census, *Statistical Abstracts of the United States: 1966*, 87th edition (Washington, D.C., 1966), Table No. 3, pp. 6–7.

[2] Henry D. Sheldon, "The Changing Demographic Profile," in Clark Tibbits, ed., *Handbook of Social Gerontology: Societal Aspects of Aging* (Chicago, University of Chicago Press, 1960), p. 50.

proportionate increase in the aged population cohort in the foreseeable future, the sheer numerical increase in old people, as a function of the general growth in population size, ensures that family and other problems of the aged will be of increasing concern in the years ahead. For by 1985 the population may well contain some 24.9 million old people.

For present purposes the most significant aspect of the trend in age structure is the progressive imbalance in the sex ratio among those 65 years and over which has been occurring throughout this century. In 1910 there were 101.2 males per 100 females age 65 and over in the population. By 1940 the ratio of males to females among the aged had dropped to 95.7, and by 1960 to 82.8. This trend shows no sign of abating; in 1965 there were 77.6 males per 100 females among the aged.[3] And for the future, there is no reason to expect the imbalance to redress itself. As a consequence, the dissolution of the conjugal family emerges as a problematic feature of life in the later years not only because of the greater prominence of the aged cohort in the larger society, but also because of the sex-related trends which are occurring independently of sheer growth in size of the older population. Not only do women at any age have lower mortality rates than men, but their life expectancy is increasing more rapidly. We shall continue to see, then, an increasing surplus of older women in the population. The impact of this surplus on the family life of old people will doubtless also become increasingly severe since wives typically continue to be younger than their husbands. The disruptive impact of widowhood is already a major factor in the lives of women over 65 and its severity increases with advancing old age. In 1965 about 12 percent of all men between the ages of 65 and 74 were widowed, as compared to 44 percent of the women that age. In the next decades of life, however, widowhood rises sharply. Among men who are 75 years or over, 34 percent have lost a spouse, and fully 71 percent of the women have become widows. Looking at the matter from the viewpoint of conjugal families which have remained intact, almost three-fifths of the men 75 years or over are still married, but only one-fifth of the women remain with spouses.[4] Thus, while felt by both sexes, the effects of widowhood fall most heavily on women of advanced age. A larger proportion of all old women are bereft, and more important, a larger proportion of women than men are likely to remain so. For remarriage rates are lower for women than for men—after age 55 men

---

[3] U.S. Bureau of the Census, *op. cit.*, Table No. 19, p. 22.

[4] *Ibid.*, Table No. 32, p. 31.

tend to remarry at a rate about five times greater than women. By any measure, the family situation of old people, especially old women, involves to an acute degree the dissolution of the conjugal bond with relatively small possibility of reinstituting satisfying nuptial relationships.

It is not surprising, then, that in recent years much interest has developed in alternate forms of the family for the aged. Since the demographic realities severely limit the possibility of monogamous remarriage of an elderly widow with an age peer, attention has been directed to polygynous marriage as one possible solution to the problems of the bereft female in old age. Does polygyny offer the elderly widow in contemporary American society the opportunity to re-establish meaningful conjugal relations? Can a society which institutionalizes monogamy as the sole form of marriage accommodate itself to polygynous unions among members of a particular subgroup? What consequences for the elderly, and for their kith and kin, might ensue from the establishment of polygynous unions? Of course, it is not possible to elucidate these issues and their many ramifications without much more knowledge of the family systems of the elderly than we now possess. Still, in considering the implications of new models of the family for the elderly, it may be worthwhile to discuss some of the social bases on which alternatives to monogamy may rest and to make some observations about possible social functions of marriage alternatives for the elderly.

Marriage in Society

A comprehensive review of the forms of kinship in all societies for which data exist on the extent and scope of polygyny as compared to monogamy has led one observer [5] to note a seeming paradox. On the one hand, there is no question that monogamy is characteristic of almost all societies, since monogamous unions are almost without exception the most *frequent* type of marriage in any given society. But on the other hand, in the overwhelming majority of societies, polygyny is the *preferred* form and does appear in fact within all of these societies— although not with modal frequency. Apparently, then, in most societies it is not possible to arrive at the conditions which are necessary to main-

[5] George Peter Murdock, *Social Structure* (New York, The Free Press, 1965), pp. 27–28. The discussion of the economic conditions associated with different marriage forms draws heavily on Murdock.

tain the desired form as the most frequently realized form of marriage. One of the necessary conditions germane to the situation of the elderly concerns the economy and the division of labor by sex in society.

The form of marriage in a society depends to a considerable extent on whether the economic roles of women permit a husband to enjoy a significant economic advantage as a right in his wife. Where the division of labor by sex in a society is such that women make little or no contribution to the economy, the rewards accruing to a polygynous family may be outweighed by the burden imposed on the husband in order to support additional spouses. For example, in such situations household tasks may be allotted to men. In these societies, the likelihood of polyandrous marriage is probably highest. Where the division of labor between the sexes approaches equality, and therefore where both small and large families are about equally efficient, the likelihood of monogamous marriage is probably highest. But where the division of labor is such that the contribution a woman can make to the economy of the family is relatively large, and where, in addition, a man can produce a surplus beyond what he needs to support himself, additional wives may become real economic assets. By taking multiple spouses a man may maintain a precarious economic position or even improve the economic standing of his family. Under such circumstances, polygyny may be the preferred and the practiced form of marriage. It should be said, however, that the occurrence of polygyny under these conditions mainly has been confined to African societies. In many other parts of the world, polygynous forms of marriage have appeared largely among the wealthy in a given society, or among chiefs where numerous wives were signs of success and therefore conferred great prestige.

The preference for, and realization of, polygynous unions, is affected by another condition, one which is in part rooted in the economic structure of a society and in part independent of it. This is the existence of a counter-ideology. A recent comprehensive study of the relation between marriage and the family as social institutions and the world-wide modernization and industrialization of contemporary societies places particular emphasis on the ideology of the conjugal family as a major factor in the declining prevalence of polygyny throughout the world.[6] The main components of this world-wide

[6] William J. Goode, *World Revolution and Family Patterns* (New York, The Free Press, 1963), p. 377 *et passim*.

cultural trend include increasing freedom of choice of spouse, stronger emphasis on equalitarianism in the marriage relationship, and perhaps most important of all, a higher evaluation of the emotional qualities of the conjugal relation. Hence there has emerged a general unwillingness to tolerate the participation of other wives in family life. This general process of change in values concerning the family, it should be stressed, is not necessarily the result of industrialization, but rather has been viewed as an accompanying trend—and in some instances may even be considered a prelude to industrialization and modernization of a society.

To what extent are these basic structural and cultural conditions apposite to the situation of the elderly in American society today? In the first place, the retirement of the older male from the economy, whether voluntary or forced, is consequential for the division of labor by sex. Retirement deprives the older breadwinner of his chief role, as has been noted often in discussions of so-called "role losses" of the aged. But in addition, and more significant in its implications for possible new forms of the family in old age, retirement disrupts the division of labor by sex within the family. The *family* economy is altered in such a way that the preponderance of "work" which contributes to the physical maintenance of the household shifts to the direct effort the wife contributes to domestic chores. The male's indirect contribution to the household economy, represented by the goods and services purchased through wages and salary, is either drastically reduced or ceases altogether. The approximate symmetry in the allocation of roles between the homemaker and the breadwinner becomes transformed into an asymmetrical division of labor in which the contribution of the wife is relatively more substantial. She still performs most of the household tasks, as in the past, but her husband's role in the household economy has been reduced from provider to part-time household assistant. (This may or may not be viewed as a comfortable arrangement by the participants; but the question of satisfaction and morale is not at issue at this point.) And should the wife herself hold some employment, or receive some pension funds from past employment, or simply represent an additional economic benefit by virtue of her legal status as a "dependent," then this only serves to intensify the asymmetry of the division of labor by increasing still further the relative amount of the wife's contribution to the family economy. In this sense, some of the structural conditions underlying monogamy begin to be undermined at the onset of old age. The approximate equality of the division of labor by sex, which during the child-rearing and working years of the life cycle supports the monogamous form of the family, has been altered so that the family economy could possibly accommodate polygynous marriage—other things being equal.

From the perspective of the older widow as a potential economic asset within family context, remarriage in widowhood does nothing to redress the balance in the division of labor by sex. Quite the contrary, the widow's value in the wider marriage market may in fact be enhanced. Property may have accrued to her by inheritance, adding as it were an inadvertent dowry to her value as housekeeper and homemaker. It is reasonable to estimate that at the time of the death of a spouse, about 75 percent of the newly widowed in the United States own homes, and at that point must choose whether to keep them. A recent nation-wide survey of the aged finds large proportions of non-married older women had elected to maintain home ownership after the death of a spouse. Among the entire population of widows, about half of those between the ages of 62 and 72 remain homeowners, and two-fifths of all widows 73 years old and over maintain possession of their homes.[7] Moreover, the median income, excluding contributions from other members of their family, of widows who own their homes (whether or not they share them with relatives) is likely to be higher than that of non-homeowning widows.[8] And furthermore, there is some evidence to suggest that since 1951 the proportion of widows with relatives in their households has been declining.[9] Thus, in terms of their worth as partners in marriage, a fairly large proportion of older widows represent non-negligible assets in and of themselves due to home ownership and income apart from what is received from other family members. And should the possibility of remarriage occur, it is becoming less likely that older widows would be disrupting the living arrangements of other relatives with whom they pool resources in a common home. Some fairly substantial proportion of widows, then, do not in fact constitute a population of total dependents. The structure of the family economy in polygynous unions would not in all cases necessarily entail deficit financing—at least not at the outset of polygynous family formation.

---

[7] Janet Murray, Donald M. Pilcher, and L. D. Platky, "Living Arrangements of the Aged," *1963 Survey of the Aged*. Publication of the Office of Research and Statistics, Social Security Administration (Washington, D.C., October, 1965), p. 10.

[8] *Ibid.*, p. 18.

[9] *Ibid.*, p. 24.

Thus, some of the conditions exist in old age which are not incompatible with plural marriage. These conditions concern certain relations between the family and the economy. The division of economic labor by sex within the conjugal unit as well as the economic value of potential additional spouses do not of themselves preclude polygynous family formation.

However, since marriage is the unique institutional arrangement which combines economic and sexual-emotional relationships, it is not enough to note merely the economic conditions conducive to alternate forms of the family. The values governing the quality of the conjugal relationship also weigh heavily in any assessment of potential for family transformation in old age. And unlike economic roles and resources, which may shift with age, the values associated with family life appear to remain stable through the many vicissitudes of aging. Indeed, the retention into old age of value orientations toward conjugal family relationships is simply one facet of a more general feature of the interpersonal relationships of the aged. That is, the behavior and values of old people are to a large extent a continuation of the patterns which characterized their middle age and their youth.

The available evidence on the maintenance of the conjugal values of earlier years into old age is scant, but the direction in which it points is unmistakable. There are indications that the current generation of older people were themselves reared in families which socialized them to affectionate conjugal norms and values, as opposed to those values congruent with more traditional extended family forms. And they continue to adhere to these values in their own old age after children have left home—and even after social distance between the generations has increased through upward occupational mobility of their offspring.[10] Moreover, widowhood itself does not result in alteration of the balance of remaining affectional family bonds. Widowhood, for example, does not result in an increased emotional dependency on children; for people widowed in old age are no more dependent than those whose spouse is still alive.[11] Even when it may appear as if sharp role reversals in the emotional aspects of conjugal relations have occurred in old age, closer scutiny usually reveals that it is rather a lifelong manifestation of

[10] Gordon F. Streib and Wayne E. Thompson, "The Older Person in a Family Context," in Clark Tibbits, ed., *Handbook of Social Gerontology, op. cit.*, pp. 482–483.
[11] Irving Rosow, *Social Integration of the Aged* (New York, The Free Press, 1967), p. 206 *et passim*.

personality and value which "... has emerged with greater clarity at this time than it has at others." [12] And one investigator feels confident enough of the persistence of prior orientations to generalize from the relations of older married women and older widows with their children to broader realms of the social life of the aged: "there may be no effective substitute for the loss of any major social role except an equally significant status which is as highly valued and rewarded." [13]

Therefore, it seems fair to state that although polygynous marriage in principle may provide an alternative to the status of monogamous spouse, it is neither regarded as significant nor rewarded by the predominantly conjugal values which are retained from earlier socialization to, and experience in, monogamy. The ideological stress on egalitarianism in the conjugal relation, the emphasis on women's right to choose a husband, and the romantic love pattern which assumes that because a husband loves his wife, she has a certain degree of influence over him, would all appear to militate against polygynous marriage for the aged.[14] Thus, the marital status highly valued in Western societies today does not seem to fit with the role of polygynist as a realistic substitute for that of monogamous spouse.

Functions of Alternate Family Models for the Aged

The preceding remarks suggest that there are certain categories of functions which should be considered when weighing the implications of alternate forms of marriage for the aged. For example, while there is no question that polygynous marriage in old age might be economically advantageous, polygyny in one segment of a monogamous society also may have economic consequences through its effect on kinship ties with the younger generation. The relationship under question is a complex one, but perhaps some of the underlying issues can be clarified by focusing briefly on one facet of the problem for purposes of illustration. Consider inheritance.

---

[12] Alvin I. Goldfarb, "Psychodynamics and the Three-Generation Family," in Ethel Shanas and Gordon F. Streib, eds., *Social Structure and the Family: Generational Relations* (Englewood Cliffs, N.J., Prentice-Hall, 1965), p. 45.

[13] Rosow, *op. cit.*, p. 245.

[14] See, e.g., Goode, *op. cit.*, pp. 18–21.

Under most jurisdictions in the United States, when no will has been made, a surviving spouse in the presence of children is usually entitled to a third of the estate. When a will has been made, so strong is the concern in law for a surviving spouse that he or she cannot be freely disinherited in most states.[15] The legal norms of our society reflect great interest in the fiscal integrity of the *entire* conjugal family. The equalitarian distribution of property rights within the family of procreation is one mechanism whereby the class position of *all* conjugal family members may be preserved or enhanced. Dispersion of inheritance within the conjugal family helps to keep the class system fluid by insuring some equality of advantage among family members, yet it does not rend the conjugal family system by dissipating its collective resources to the outside. However, if widowhood and subsequent polygynous remarriage effectively transfers some proportion of the accumulated wealth of one family to another lineage, then the integration of the conjugal family system across generations is weakened. The question is not one of maintaining a lineage, it should be understood, but rather it is one involving an adjustive mechanism mediating between the family system and the economy. And one consequence of polygyny in old age is that it may alter such a mechanism so that invidious class considerations disrupt kinship relations and some added measure of rigidity is introduced into the class system.

But polygynous models of the family for the aged also should be considered in the light of their implications for the emotional aspects of family cohesion, and for family values as these are manifest in interaction among kin. Research has only recently begun to disclose the extent of the role of the aged within the family context. Recent studies reveal that the two most important centers of kin involvement in urban families are females and the aged.[16] And the role of the grandparental generation emerges as particularly important in interpersonal relations within the kinship network. The aged are a key factor in maintaining social relationships between the major parts of the family network. They link siblings of their own nuclear family of procreation together. They maintain connections among their own siblings and their siblings'

[15] Max Rheinstein, "Motivation of Intergenerational Behavior by Norms of Law," in Shanas and Streib, *op. cit.*, pp. 258–259.

[16] See, e.g., Bert N. Adams, *Kinship in an Urban Setting* (Chicago, Markham Publishing Co., 1968), pp. 17–32, 167.

children. And they serve to integrate the family of procreation with the family of orientation, not only in terms of mutual interaction, but also by keeping kin informed of each other's activities. The link between the widowed mother and her daughter is particularly important. Children, of course, give aid to a widowed mother, but a daughter also receives substantial assistance in turn. Furthermore, the married daughter and her widowed mother share activities in addition to reciprocal aid. The daughter sees her relationship with her widowed mother as obligatory to some extent, but the enjoyment she derives from the relationship is more important in her mind. The married daughter in fact is more likely to maintain patterned social relationships and organizational attendance with her widowed mother than when her father was alive.[17] Thus it can be seen that the aged in a family context are much more than symbols of bilateral unity; they are active agents of that unity and of family integration for they play an important expressive role throughout a wide sector of the network of kin. The consequence of polygynous remarriage of the older widow for the expressive integration of the family would seem to be a considerable weakening of unity within the kin network. The degree of obligation felt by family members to interact with the aged would have a weaker basis in reality since presumably the older family member is adequately cared for in her remarriage. And it is conceivable that the amount of family interaction which is undertaken because it is enjoyable, as in mother-daughter activities, would be reduced. That is, if by analogy with fiscal capital one can look at expressive capital and its circulation within the family system, polygynous remarriage in old age might have an effect parallel to that hypothesized above in connection with the economic resources of the aged: it might be drained off into other lineage, thus contributing to the emotional impoverishment of the family.

Summary

The demography of old age poses a problem concerning the family structure of the aged. The aged have increased as a proportion of the population at the same time as the sex ratio has become progressively imbalanced. In the United States today, and in the foreseeable future,

---

[17] *Ibid.*, pp. 86–88.

there is an evergrowing surfeit of old widows. Under these conditions, what are the implications of polygynous marriage in old age?

The foregoing remarks called attention to two conditions which appear to accompany polygynous marriage systems: an economic division of labor by sex in which the contribution of the female is substantial, and the absence of a counter-ideology. With respect to the first condition, it was pointed out that the population of widows in the United States represents considerable assets, which, coupled with the retirement role of the male, weights the female contribution to the family economy in old age relatively more heavily than during the working years of the breadwinner. But while in a structural, economic, sense polygyny thus seems possible, this favorable condition is offset by the existence of a counter-ideology—the ideology of the conjugal family—which everywhere in the modern world is gaining ascendance. This ideology is inimical to polygynous family formation. In addition, there is no reason to suspect that the aging female can or will abandon the monogamous values to which she was initially socialized.

Finally, it was noted that the redistribution of assets outside of an original family lineage, which is implicit in polygynous marriage in old age, would tend to disrupt kinship relations and introduce an element of rigidity in the class system. And polygyny also would tend to divert the energies of old people from an important expressive role they play in integrating the family network.

Epilogue

This is indeed an age of great and positive change. We are on the threshold of entering the era of the innovative society. Certainly the pre-conditions for such an era exist. For the first time in history, extensive and highly workable "tools," methods, and theoretical frameworks have been forged which enable us to more fully understand the genesis and functioning of personality. More important, we are now more clearly aware *that we can help man to continue to grow as a person throughout his entire life span so that he can actualize more of his vast potential.* With our increasing understanding of inter-personal as well as group processes and dynamics, has come recognition that the group can function as a medium of personality growth not only for patients, but for effective and productive people. Elucidation of group and inter-personal processes, in turn, has given us greater insight into the nature of relationships within institutions and institutional structures. Thus, man is finally at a point where he is capable of structuring his relationships and institutions—or, alternatively, freeing them from rigid structure—to insure the highest possible fulfillment for the individuals involved.

While there have always been rebels, while there have always been controversial individuals or groups of individuals, man is now for the first time capable of establishing creative relationships and institutions not in defiance of society, or in lonely isolation from it, but in co-existence with it. For the first time, individually tailored living/loving arrangements are possible not only for the exceptional man, the "wrong or odd number," but for the healthy well-functioning individual who seeks neither notoriety nor superficial "thrills" but the warmth and intimacy of deep loving relationships with persons he cherishes.

Certainly there are many indications that in all too many instances the institutions of marriage and the family, *as they exist now*, do not offer sufficient warmth, intimacy, and deep loving. The institution is in need of strengthening. New forms of relationship and new ways of being can be found and developed *within* existing marriage and family structures. At the same time, we need to encourage and support open experimentation, with new relationship forms, new forms of togetherness and closeness, and new patterns of relatedness for purposes of companionship and child-rearing. We are now beginning to realize that *all* social systems are in need of change. John Gardner, in his books *Self Renewal* and *Excellence*, uses the terms social and institutional regeneration. If we accept the notion that the primary purpose of the institution is to aid in the actualization of human potential, we are confronted with a question: "How and in what ways do we need to re-shape, develop, and regenerate our institutions so that they will enable man to realize more of his potentialities?" Or, to put it differently, how shall we re-structure our institutions in terms of the kinds of social relatedness which we need to develop? Perhaps the key question here is *what kinds of social relatedness are experienced as personally stimulating and growthful, as fulfilling and unfolding, as re-affirming authenticity and integrity, as supportive, creative, and loving?*

The task of institutional regeneration is complicated by the fact that technologically we have attained such a level of destructiveness, in our present society, that man may very well extinguish himself from earth as a species. The race is between self-destruction and institutional regeneration. According to one unpublished report, small nations will have atomic weapons as well as the even more destructive armamentarium of biological warfare within the very near future. It is expected that with the rapid advance of technology, even large criminal gangs and syndicates will have access to this weaponry. Given the level of generalized hostility rampant in our society plus the implicit doctrine of mutual exploitation which permeates vast segments of social inter-action, it is very clear that we must initiate massive social change before generalized hostility and species-destructive weaponry wipe us out.

A further complication is added by the unbelievably far-advanced poisoning of man's natural environment, including the ionosphere, through the waste products of technology. Man is literally poisoning himself as he is poisoning the planet and atmosphere which has cradled him, and shaped his being. An intricate and symbiotic relationship exists between man and his environment; they form an ecological system, an inseparable and inter-dependent dynamic force and growth field. We are dependent on the plants (and animals) for our survival. Yet many scientists are now in agreement that the natural processes by which oxygen is replenished through green plants is imperiled.

Pollution of the atmosphere by the combustion engine, by industrial waste, and by the destruction of vegetation by building and paving of earth surfaces is endangering the earth's oxygen supply. Man and his planet are a life form—a total living organism. Man and nature are part of the same ecological system. If enough destructive change is introduced into nature, destructive processes are set in motion in man.

As one of the most technologically advanced nations, the United States contributes massively, not only to the poisoning of its own population but to the poisoning of the planet. Paradoxically, laws exist in most states to prohibit this wholesale poisoning of rivers, lakes, and seashore by industry. *It speaks to the dysfunction of our governmental institutions* that special interests (oil, steel, chemical, and other major industrial complexes) are allowed to continue poisoning the atmosphere and environment of *all* citizens. For the profit of the very few, everyone suffers. Perhaps if the directors of these companies in each and every locality, those directly responsible for blighting the lives of their fellow men, were publicly identified, social pressure might be brought to bear so that we could regain clear air, clear rivers and lakes, and unpolluted beaches which are our birthright.

More fundamentally, what is desperately needed is the regeneration of our democratic institutions and processes. Our system has degenerated into an oligarchy in which power élites pay little heed to the wishes and needs of the citizens. The playing of ego and status games, and the jockeying to obtain handouts for special interests, too often characterize our elected leaders or "politicians."

When we look at this massive accumulation of factors and forces which threaten to destroy man we must again question whether contemporary social structures, and particularly the institutions of marriage and the family as they exist today, function in ways to insure man's survival. Certainly the facts about our despoiled environment and the accumulation of species-destructive "defense" weaponry are widely known. Yet it is also clear that the contemporary marriage and family have not been able to generate enough loving and caring in their members, either for themselves or for their fellow man, to mobilize their strength and to assume responsibility for the bringing about of constructive social change. *The contemporary marriage and family structure, cradled in other institutions themselves in need of regeneration, does not seem able to produce enough loving, caring, socially responsible citizens to reverse man's self-destructive course.* This is one of the most cogent arguments in favor of our fostering and supporting experimentation with different relationships and family forms. Unquestionably, the socially responsible, politically active college and high school generation of today is our greatest hope. But this is not enough, and may be a case of "too little and too late."

To effect true social regeneration we need to encourage responsible dialogue leading to innovation and experimentation with new forms of social and communal living. Sociologists, psychologists, and others who have considered non-traditional forms of marriage and family life generally seem to concur with each other and most of the authors cited in this book, that the majority of individuals living in this society, at this time, would most likely choose monogamous living were they given free choice from a variety of alternatives. This, of course, does nothing to obviate the rights of the minority who might choose other relationship forms—nor does it preclude the possibility of another generation adhering less exclusively to these traditional forms.

If it is admitted that individuals do, in fact, have the right to the "pursuit of happiness," so long as they do not infringe upon the rights of others, then it follows logically that alternative marriage and family forms which do not injure others should not only be permitted but encouraged.

Repeating our earlier assumption that this is potentially an age of great and positive change, we must emphasize that all necessary changes have *not* been made—and *will* not be made, unless society in general, and its leaders in particular, accept the challenge offered them by an increased awareness of man's infinite and rich potential.

Appendix

The Group Family: A New Social Concept

For thousands of years world religions have been preaching at us to "Love one another." Indeed, it is only through loving human relations that mankind can solve its conflicts and problems, evolve materially and spiritually, and discover happiness. Yet, how can we translate this affection into practical social and economic structures? So far, the bonds of blood-ties (kinship, the family) and marriage have been the main ones to express this relationship. Useful as these two forms may be, human affection can express itself through yet other forms which extend and complement these two.

Most people would agree that not all brothers and sisters are of the same character, temperament, and outlook, nor need they necessarily all get on well together. This also applies to relationships between parents and grown-up sons or daughters, between whom there are years of change and different modes of thinking and living. Also, with the need for mobility of labor, families often have to separate. In such a situation, the individual can find himself or herself alone, probably in a big city, having only superficial contacts, but not deep or meaningful ones. Such an isolated individual can become a prey to loneliness, alcoholism, nervous breakdown, political propaganda, or anti-social behavior.

As for marriage, the picture of a conventional family today is that of a couple with one or two children, bravely battling against the rest of the world. This most ingenious artificial institution, grafted onto certain basic human needs (material security, sex, companionship, the protection of children, etc.) serves those who control society: it is a way to "divide and rule." Because of that, and the preservation of property within the narrow limits of the family circle, the Establishment, to promote its own interests, tries to impose the concept of the conventional family through school, home, mass media, pulpit, etc., not to mention the violence of the law.

We challenge this concept. We do not believe that such a narrow definition of the family does good in the long run either to members of the family or to society as a whole. We do not think that institutionalized selfishness is a good thing. We believe that a man or woman is capable of loving more than one's own biological child, as is evidenced in many cases of child adoption, foster parents, and godparents. Similarly, it is possible, in fact socially desirable, for a man to love more than one woman, and for a woman to love more than one man. Marriage does not exhaust, and should not cripple, the person's ability to express affection toward others. If we see these two or more loves as opposed or contradictory, it is because we have been conditioned from childhood to accept blindly a narrow and crippling definition of the words "family" and "marriage." We do not wish to destroy the concept of family, but to enrich and enlarge it, so as to include other men, women and children with whom we are in natural affinity. In some cases, the relationship could have a sexual side, in others not (e.g., elderly ladies who feel sisterly toward each other and live together as such). There are immense material and practical benefits that result from the group family system, and even greater psychological and spiritual advantages. Finally, from the social point of view, such a group, which shares and pools not only its incomes, assets, skills and facilities, but also its ideas, feelings, joys, sorrows, experiences, and ideals, can promote a happier and better society and way of life. This is real Christianity, real Humanism, real Communism, not the pale imitations which are being sold to us today as such.

Child adoption is widely accepted. Adults too could "adopt" each other, with favorable results for all concerned, for are they less in need of caring and sharing, of loving and being loved? The Group Family is a social expression of that need, and mutual aid for the welfare of all. Must such positve, humane, and creative relations be limited only to the marriage vows and discouraged outside them?

When two or more persons have known each other over a period of time, have discovered common bonds and affinities, and gained affection for each other, they may form a Group Family to give more definite shape to their relationship, and to encourage its expression into deeper and more meaningful channels. In the Group Family, or mutual adult adoption, there is no mine and thine, but "ours": our home (a community flat or house), our common fund, our children. Thus we can find happiness through sharing and serving, and live at a deeper level which removes the root causes of much personal and social suffering through isolation. Most of our social evils are the result of our present mistaken concepts and poor human relations, which make strangers of our fellow humans. The Group Family may, in some cases, imply Group Marriage, in the practical if not the legal sense. The family should not be a strait-jacket where too intensive and sometimes explosive relations exist, but a cooperative group sharing a similar outlook on life, always open to include other suitable persons. Older members act in the role of uncles, aunts, or grand-parents. The younger adults can function as spouses.

Although apparently revolutionary, the idea and practice are not new. They have been successfully applied for many years, with local variations, in the Polynesian islands, in African communities, in Israeli kibbutzim, among the Eskimos, etc. This way of life is currently practiced by some hippies and others in the U.S.A. and the U.K., and by increasing numbers of young people in Sweden.

Our present social units may have been suitable for other times and other social conditions. Many of these have become outdated in the twentieth century. We have to free ourselves from the old ways of thinking and living, and look at the present situation with fresh, objective eyes. No one has the right to dictate to others how they shall live, as long as they cause no physical harm to others. We believe that the path to world harmony begins in the home—now. The segre-gation of small families from each other and from the community must give way to integration. The decay or destruction of our de-humanized society may be the price we will have to pay, if we lack the courage and imagination to adopt new social structures. The spread of inter-linked Group Family units could well provide a frame-work for a better social order, which would deal with the problem of human alienation and breakdown in our times. It would also contain and express the spiritual values of the various idealistic and religious movements.

Cold Mountain Farm[1]

Given: 450 acres of land, twelve usable for farming or pasture, the remainder being old, neglected apple orchards (also pear, plum, and cherry trees) and young woods, in a mountainous upstate New York

[1] Joyce Gardener, "The Cold Mountain Farm," *Modern Utopian* (August 1967); reprinted through the assistance of the publisher.

dairy-farming area. A beautiful piece of land, with three running streams in the springtime, but only one good spring for water in the summer, close to the five-bedroomed house. The farm is one mile off the main road, at the end of a rugged dirt road, a mile from the closest neighbor. There is no rent, no electricity, no telephone—and to acquire any of these would be extremely costly.

The Group: Anarchists. Mostly in their twenties, with children under six. A fluctuating population, up to thirty. About four couples and one or two single people consider this home. Mostly former residents of NYC, but some from other parts of the East Coast. Interrelationships have existed for as long as five years.

History: Goes back two and a half years, to NYC, where a communal loft once existed, with shared dinners and other occasions. Or back three years, when at least two families shared an apartment together for a few months. Or to last spring and summer, when a group of NYC anarchists used half an acre of a friend's land to farm on weekends.

More concretely, June 1966, to a "Community Conference" at the School of Living in Heathcote, Md., out of which emerged a new community—"Sunrise Hill"—at Conway, Mass. At least one person, loosely connected with the NYC anarchists, went to live there.

The rest of us continued to farm our friend's land on weekends during the summer, meeting at least once a month at different places in the country during the winter—living together for a few days, getting to know one another better, and making plans to start our own farm the following spring. Some people from Sunrise Hill also attended these meetings.

We finally located this place through a friend. About that time, Sunrise Hill was suffering its final collapse—due to internal conflicts— and four people from there eventually would join us.

Onto the Land

Starting a community farm is an incredibly difficult thing. We didn't fully realize this when we began. Setting up a new farm—or rather, rehabilitating an old and neglected one—was at least a season's work. Not to mention compensating for the work which should have been done the previous autumn.

It was still cold, there was occasional snow, the house was difficult to heat, and no one was prepared to move in. The dirt road was all but impassable, we walked the mile through snow and later mud—carrying babies, supplies, bedding, etc.

Meanwhile we had to find a tractor immediately to haul manure for compost heaps. They should have been started the year before as they require three months' time to rot properly and we wanted to farm organically. We'd have to prune the neglected fruit trees within a month, since pruning too late in the season would shock them.

On the many rainy days we had to make the house liveable: build shelves, worktable, bookshelves, a tool shed, a mail box; install a sink; acquire tools and materials. Somehow, whatever needed to be done, there was always someone who knew how to do it or who was willing to find out how. But with each person having some particular responsibility upon himself, there wasn't time to work on group projects.

Well, we had a farm, didn't we? All we had to do was go there when it got nice and warm, plow the land, plant our seed, and wait for the vegetables to come. We didn't even have to pay any rent! It was so simple. No rush to get out there while it was still so cold.

Consequently, the farm was completely deserted until the end of April. Then news got out fast (we couldn't help but brag a little), and we found we had hundreds of friends who wanted to "come to the country." So we had to bite our tongues and violate all the laws of lower east side hospitality to avoid creating a youth hostel or a country resort. We lost a lot of friends that way.

Meanwhile, in NYC, an infinite number of conflicts existed growing out of two difficult years of co-existence, trying to work out an ideology based on anarchism-community-ecology-technology in an environment which presented a constant contradiction to it.

We had discouraged the city people. No one came. The land cried out to be tended, but people were preoccupied with their own personal grievances. The farm was all but deserted. The work fell entirely on the shoulders of a few people. Without telephone and often without car, we waited daily for friends and supplies to show up; waiting for reinforcements. Finally three friends arrived from Conway, reassuringly bringing all their worldly goods. The man started out at once, hooking up running water in the house, pruning some apple trees, then driving to a nearby town without a license or proper registration, and spending three days in jail. Soon he bought us a much-needed tractor. It was precisely this tractor (to this day still only half payed for) which shuttled up and down the one-mile dirt road, hauling cow shit (from neighboring farms, who proved surprisingly friendly) and transporting little children to the nearby town in lieu of Hershey bars—and then, as the time to plow grew nigh, flatly refused to budge.

There was absolutely nothing anyone could do. We had to wait for our friend from Florida to return. He was our only mechanic. Days passed and finally a few people started digging their own gardens —such a pathetic task for a farm that hoped to support some thirty people and then give out free food in the city.

But all this time there were small compensations. We had an opportunity now to explore this incredible land, watch the seasons change, see the snow melt and trees slowly push forth buds, see birds moving in and laying eggs; spy on porcupines each night loudly chomping on the house, make friends with cows and four wild horses grazing on neighboring fields, start to know one another in that unique way that only comes from living together.

Tribal Feelings

Now a few more old friends began to arrive. There was an incredible feeling of warmth, of family. We were becoming a tribe. There were long, good discussions, around the fire, into the night. Slowly, things were beginning to take shape. In those days I loved to look into the "community room," and see a bunch of people sprawled out on cushions around the floor, all so brown, their bodies so well-developed, their faces relaxed, naked or wearing clothes often of their own making. You could always spot someone from the city—by the whiteness of their flesh, the tenseness of their body.

It was my dream—and certainly no one openly disagreed with me—to become a tribe, a family of "incestuous brothers and sisters." Unfortunately, living so close, we probably made love less than when we lived in separate apartments in the city. And there was so much fear and tension in the air about *potential* affairs, that actual love-making all too seldom took place, and even physical contact became a rare thing. Even though we created our own environment at the farm, we still carried with us the repressions of the old environment, in our bodies and our minds.

While others were not actually opposed to these ideas, most people didn't feel quite ready for them, and certainly no one else bespoke the same vision. If we could find a form by which our visions could be shared. . . .

Incredible Tractor

Waiting for the tractor to be fixed (it took about a week and a half of hard labor), living our usual lives, making our own bread and yogurt, etc., we spoke to a nearby farmer and learned of a barn full of manure which he paid men to haul away for him. We offered to do it for him free, in exchange for manure to use as compost. He was so overjoyed that he offered to come up and plow our land in exchange for our labor. We thought he was joking, but a couple of days later, we heard a loud and unfamiliar motor coming up the hill, and there was that huge, incredible tractor. "Well, where do you want it?" And that's how we got six acres of land plowed and harrowed (later, we would plow a couple of acres ourselves). A couple of days later, we got our own tractor fixed in order to start hauling manure and planting at a furious pace, trying to get the crops in before it was too late. We were already at least a week behind most everyone else in the area . . . in a place with a *very short* growing season.

These people were so overwhelmingly happy to finally have the tractor, after weeks of frustrated waiting and digging by hand, that one person actually planted some forty mounds of zuchini and eighty mounds of acorn squash and several rows of corn in one day, by hand! Then he devised a method whereby he could dig five furrows at a time by building a drag with teeth for the tractor, and installing the three women as weights on the drag, where they could drop onion sets into the rows. That last part didn't work so well (all the onion sets had to be spaced again, by hand), but nonetheless, by the time the other folks got home about a week later, close to an acre of land had been planted.

Now that there were more of us, we were not so close. There was no real sense of community between us. There was good feeling, but no center, no clear-cut purpose. Some of the men felt an unfulfilled need to fight. The women felt an unfulfilled need to love.

About this time we undertook—or were overtaken by—what I consider one of our most challenging feats: trying to assimilate a young lawyer and his family, including two girls, aged four and six. Many a group meeting centered around the problem of "the kids." Because they were breaking out of a sick environment, their parents felt they needed a maximum of patience and love and understanding. Others felt they needed simply to be treated as human beings and that their mother should not repress the anger and frustration which she obviously felt.

Most of us felt we should in fact try to let them work *through* their hangups and hopefully eventually come out the other side. Let them yell "penis" and "vagina" at the top of their lungs. Let them throw Raggedy Anne into the cellar and elaborate upon her tortures while chanting, "No, you *can't* come out of the cellar!" all day long. But what no one seemed to be able to endure were the howls and wails which rose from the lungs of one sister after the other, time after time, all day long, and particularly on rainy days, of which there were many, locked up with them in the house all day long.

Apparently we just weren't strong enough nor healthy enough ourselves to be able to cope with these children. And their parents, who had had such great hopes of finding in us a healthy environment, soon had to build their own shelter in order to remove themselves from our environment.

By this time the house had become so generally unbearable that everyone else as well had decided to move out. Just before then, there had been twenty adults and ten children—with only three or four adults and one child sleeping outside—living so close together in that house. It seemed absurd to try to keep the house clean (anarchism does not necessarily mean chaos). And the flies were so bad that if we hung five strips of flypaper fresh each day in each room, by evening they were dripping with puddles of gooey flies. It was just barely possible to exist in the midst of all these copulating multitudes. (We didn't like the idea of using poison sprays, with all the cats and babies.)

And so, in a burst of desperation to escape the noise, children, chaos, flies, tension . . . everybody dropped everything and for a few days did nothing but work on their own shelters. The house was almost deserted.

People who get into community too often forget about the importance of solitude. And we were lucky enough to have plenty of land so that everyone could have their own shelter. But personal possessions (especially kitchen stuff), which had originally been pooled with a great sense of communal enthusiasm, were righteously carted off to their owners' shelters.

Hostile Outsiders

About this time we started coming into conflict with the outside world. Ever since it got warm, we had all been walking around more or less nude most of the time. Unfortunately, we had to discontinue this most pleasant practice when neighbors started to mention casually that they could "see everything" from their property on the hill, and that "people were talking." Our local reputation was getting progressively worse. There were too many articles in the mass media about hippies, often loosely connected with legalizing marijuana. The local people, who had originally just thought of us as "strange," and had then begun to accept us as old-fashioned organic farmers, could now call us "hippies" and forbid their kids to have anything to do with us.

The local sheriff began to take an interest in us. Whenever we went into town, we were stopped by the cops. And a friendly gas station attendant told us the highway patrol had been told to watch us. It was easy to be paranoid, to imagine their trying to take our kids away for nudity. It was terrible to compromise, but most of us began to wear clothes again. That was a great loss.

Economic Argument

I suppose our first and worst economic argument was whether or not to buy chickens. At first, it was incredible how little a problem money had been. Whoever came just threw in whatever they had— $100 or $200 perhaps—and we'd live off that until someone got a tax return, a welfare check, or whatever. We never did spend more than $25 a week on food—even when there were thirty people. But the chicken crisis involved all sorts of things. Did we need eggs (wasn't wheat germ good enough)? Was it morally right to take eggs from chickens; wasn't it cruel to keep chickens caged?—but if we didn't cage them how would we keep them out of the garden? Were we really saving money on eggs, if we had to spend money on the chickens, chicken wire, and all kinds of feed? Who was going to plant an acre of millet and an acre of corn to feed them? Who would build the chicken coop? This was the first time I remember hearing anyone say, "Well, *I* won't give any money for chickens"—using money as a weapon, a personal source of power. And it wasn't long before money again became a personal possession.

Bad Times

I liked the young lawyer and his wife because they often spoke at meetings on a personal level, about how they *felt* about things, while most of our people maintained a kind of cold objectivity, only discussing things external to themselves. It was this lack of "feeling" which brought the lawyer to say that *Cold* Mountain was certainly an apt name for the place. And his wife complained, not unjustly, that there was not enough making of music, not enough dancing, and she felt her joy was being stifled here.

We seemed to have reached an all-time low. We had passed the summer solstice. Our money was all but depleted. We could work at haying for local farmers, but $1/hr. wasn't a hell of a lot. Until now we seemed to have been subsisting mostly on enthusiasm. Now it was hot and even our enthusiasm was gone. There was a general feeling of emptiness. Times were very bad, but we tried to hold on until the times were more favorable. We decided to limit ourselves to just a few staples (rice, oil, powdered milk, soy sauce, flour, salt, soy beans, brewers yeast, molasses, grass—always purchased in huge quantities to save money) and whatever we could get from our environment—at this time of year, dandelion greens, wintergreen and burdock root and, in a little while, fresh strawberries, rhubarb and wild leeks. And we'd soon be getting edible weeds from the garden: milkweed, sorrel, lamb's quarters. And then we would discover violet leaves, for salads. Still later, there would be mushrooms, raspberries, currants and blackberries; wild mint, thyme and oregano; green apples, pears and plums—and by then we would be getting at least zuchini, peas and baby onions from the garden.

Then, one morning someone took the shotgun and killed a groundhog. We'd been talking about hunting for a long time, but most of us were vegetarians and meat was a rare sight in these parts (the hunter himself hadn't eaten meat for the last two years!). But that night he cooked up a fine groundhog stew. Which he ate. And that big pot of stew sat on the stove and people thought about it and talked about it and went to bed without dinner. In the middle of the night a couple of us woke up and had a little. Next day some of us had some for lunch. Only four people remained staunch in their vegetarianism, and mostly they didn't condemn the rest. Each of us worked it out in our own way.

Still, the diet wasn't satisfying. Subsistence living was one thing, but we all felt damned hungry. We called a meeting and decided this had a great deal to do with the cooking—which, until then, had been just a matter of chance impulse, so that the task usually fell into the hands of the same people every day. Their boredom with cooking showed up in the quality of their meals. It seemed reasonable enough that if two different people were responsible for the kitchen each day, there would be more interest and variety in cooking, the house would be kept neater and more organized, and it would leave the other people free to concentrate completely on the garden or whatever. At that time we had fourteen adults, so it was pleasant enough to know you only had to cook and clean one day/week.

It's amazing how much this helped. We'd all begun to grow so discouraged with each other and the mess we were living in. We all felt like pigs and everyone blamed the next person. Our morale was sinking fast, the kids were screaming, and we were at each other's throats. Now suddenly the house was clean—spick and span, almost. People smiled at each other again. The meals were delicious. We felt we had been reborn. We'd stuck it out through hard times, and now virtue had its reward.

At that time, four Puerto Rican friends from the city joined us. They emanated new energy and worked hard. And they had a certain revolutionary spirit which none of us quite had. One would say, "Communism and capitalism—they are both no good. But if I had something like this farm to fight for—why, I would give my life for it." At night you could hear the guitars and there were big fires, and dancing, and singing. The hardest work was over. All we had to do now was weed and mulch. Now we had time to make music.

Publicity

About this time, an article appeared about us in the *East Village OTHER*—without our knowledge or consent—claiming we needed people to help out on the farm (as if we hadn't had enough trouble discouraging people we knew from coming up!). And we were soon flooded with letters, and every two or three days a new visitor would arrive. It created terrible tensions to have to ask them to leave, to tell them it was all a mistake. And then a couple of people we *did* know arrived and announced their intention to move in. Some of us didn't want to live with these people, while others either wanted them to stay or felt we didn't have any right to ask them to leave. We had decided a long time ago that if this happened, each person in the community would just do as he felt best, and there would be no group decisions.

But how can you ask someone that you know to leave—particularly when they've brought all their things and say they have no place else to go? I think this must be a dilemma suffered by all communities. Certainly my way of dealing with it (absolute frank honesty) was far from effective. They just stayed. And stayed. And gradually, for this reason and others, the warmth and trust and sharing between us began to die. Whatever tribal or family feelings we had had were gone.

We weren't ready to define who we were; we certainly weren't prepared to define who we weren't—it was still just a matter of intuition. We had come together for various reasons—not overtly for a common idea or ideal, but primarily because there was land and there was supposed to be a "community." Even in the original community, there were people who thought of themselves (and their reason for being here) as being primarily communitarians, or primarily farmers and back-to-the-soil revolutionaries, or primarily political revolutionaries (anarchists) or "tao-archists" for whom farming and community was just one integral part of the totality, or just plain hermits who wanted to live in the woods. All of these different people managed to work together side-by-side for a while, but the fact was that there was really no shared vision.

And then still more people arrived—people we had all been looking forward to seeing. And the house was very full. And there was a lot of confusion. And it was very difficult to cook for that many people. Again, tensions began to mount. There was so little money, and now there were three or four pregnant women here, and one or two nursing mothers. Their dietary needs were very specific, and important, and the community was unable to fulfill them. They were forced to fall back on their own resources. In similar ways, one began to feel they couldn't trust the community to meet their needs, to take care of them in an emergency. There was a feeling of general malaise. The garden wasn't being weeded. The grass was growing higher and higher. Everyone felt as if everyone else was irresponsible.

In a community, things happen on such a large scale that you need the cooperation of other people in order to accomplish almost anything. But now one began to feel as if it was easier to do a thing by oneself. It was hot. Laziness had set in, very firmly. The word "failure" was being tossed around a lot. People began to just look after themselves, and to talk as if the only reason they were here was the land. The City suddenly seemed to hold a great attraction, and whenever there was a car going in, it would be filled to capacity. The young lawyer and his family finally left, quietly.

There was one ray of light in these somber times. A new couple arrived, to stay. Nobody knew them when they came, but everyone liked them at once. They brought new energies with them, and they lifted our spirits. Slowly, all the stragglers had left—empty people who had come to fill themselves, sapping our energies, needing to be taken care of and giving nothing at all—and now there were only between four and six couples and a few single people left.

Winter Approaches

So we all lived together, peaceably enough, until one night it was very cold and wet and windy, and we could smell the coming of autumn. Then it was time to begin thinking about what we'd be doing in the winter—staying here, or moving on—and making plans accordingly. Mostly we had to consider the hardship of a very cold winter, no gas or electricity, a one-mile dirt road which would probably be inaccessible because of heavy snow (even during the summer, only jeeps and 4-wheel-drive cars and trucks could climb that road).

There were five couples, three of the women were pregnant, and a fourth was nursing. The babies were due in October, November and February. The first two couples wanted to deliver their own but not take the chance of doing it here. A single girl was already building a small stone house for the winter. Another man intended to live in the big house for the winter. Almost all hoped to be here early next Spring. By this time, two couples and a girl had moved entirely into their own shelters.

The communal garden was a monstrous failure. After the original enthusiasm of planting, hardly anyone cared enough to weed the rows. (Of course, the huge amount of rain this year retarded the growth of the crops and caused the weeds to grow like crazy! and six acres is a hell of a lot of land to weed by hand. If we try again next year, we'll certainly have to get a cultivator.) At least two acres of garden were lost, either because they weren't weeded adequately, or because they were planted too late and the growing season was too short, or because there wasn't enough sun and there was too much rain, or because of the aphids, or the potato blight. . . .

We didn't become NEW people—we just became physically healthy people. We didn't find a way of sharing our visions (in fact, we didn't even have a conscious understanding of the *need* for such a thing) and we didn't have a shared vision to bring us and hold us together.

We had plowed and begun to plant the earth, but we had not pierced our own ego skins. Decay, stagnation had already set in. I went into the woods to meditate. The woods explained: it was high time we plowed the earth of this community. We must apply the blade to ourselves and cut back the outer skin to expose the pulsating flesh. And then we must harrow and pulverize the outer skin and use our egos for compost. Then, in the new flesh, we must plant the seeds of the people we wish to become.

Growth Centers and Organizations for Actualizing Human Potential

Southern California

TOPANGA CENTER FOR HUMAN
DEVELOPMENT
P.O. Box 480
Reseda, Calif. 91335

Robert J. Hill
President

KAIROS
The Ranch
P.O. Box 350
Rancho Santa Fe, Calif. 92067

Robert J. Driver
President
Taegea Kirk, Director

Northern California

ESALEN INSTITUTE
Big Sur, Calif. 93920

Michael Murphy, Pres.
Richard Price, Vice Pres.
Ben Weaver, Director

ESALEN INSTITUTE
P.O. Box 31389
San Francisco, Calif. 94131

David Baar, Director

THE CENTER
P.O. Box 3014
Stanford, Calif. 94305

David Mastrandrea
Director

INSTITUTE FOR GROUP & FAMILY STUDIES
347 Alma
Palo Alto, Calif. 94301

BERKELEY CENTER FOR HUMAN
INTERACTION
1820 Scenic
Berkeley, Calif. 94709

Trevor Hoy
Director

EXPLORATIONS INSTITUTE
P.O. Box 1254
Berkeley, Calif. 94701

James Elliott
Director

BRIDGE MOUNTAIN FOUNDATION
2011 Alba Road
Ben Lomond, Calif. 95005

201

CENTER FOR HUMAN COMMUNICATION   James Sorrells
Family Therapy Institute, Group Ctr.   Director
120 Oak Meadow Drive
Los Gatos, Calif. 95030

TAHOE INSTITUTE   Jerry Nims
P.O. Box DD   Director
South Lake Tahoe, Calif. 95705

SOCIETY FOR COMPARATIVE   Alan Watts
PHILOSOPHY, INC.   President
P.O. Box 857
Sausalito, Calif. 94965

Northwest

SEMINARS IN GROUP PROCESS   Leon J. Fine
8475 S.W. Bohmann Parkway   Director
Portland, Oregon 97223

NORTHWEST FAMILY THERAPY INSTITUTE   Karl E. Humiston
P.O. Box 94278   President
Tacoma, Wash. 98494

STAR WEATHER RANCH INSTITUTE   Josephine Price
P.O. Box 923   President
Hailey, Idaho 83333

CENTRAL STATES

OASIS: MIDWEST CENTER FOR   Robert Shapiro
HUMAN POTENTIAL   Director
Stone-Brandel Center
1439 South Michigan Avenue
Chicago, Ill. 60605

ONTOS, INC.   John D. Burton
40 South Clay   Director
Hinsdale, Ill. 60521

CENTER FOR CREATIVE INTERCHANGE   Charles L. Palmgren
602 Center Street   Executive Director
Des Moines, Iowa 50309

KOPAVI, INC.   Jon Adelsman
4841 11th Avenue South   President
Minneapolis, Minn. 55417

CAMBRIDGE HOUSE   Sandra Badtke
1900 N. Cambridge Ave.   Acting Director
Milwaukee, Wisc. 53202

AMARE: The Institute of Human Relatedness   Melvin L. Foulds
Box 108
Bowling Green, Ohio 43402

SHADYBROOK HOUSE   Donald R. Boyce
RR 1   Director
Mentor, Ohio 44060

GESTALT INSTITUTE OF CLEVELAND, INC.   Edwin C. Nevis
12921 Euclid Avenue   President
Cleveland, Ohio 44112

COMMUNICATION CENTER 1   Mel Spehn
1001 Union Blvd.
St. Louis, Mo. 63113

MIDWEST PERSONAL GROWTH CENTER   Donald M. Sundland
200 South Hanley Road   Director
Clayton, Mo. 63105

EVERGREEN INSTITUTE   Carl Hollander
3831 W. Wagon Trail Drive   Director
Littleton, Colo. 80120

HARA, INC.   Ben Goodwin
7322 Blairview   Director
Dallas, Texas

THE LAOS HOUSE   Robert R. Bryant
700 West 19th   Executive Director
Austin, Texas 78701

ESPIRTU   Leland Johnson
1214 Miramar   Director
Houston, Texas 77005

EAST COAST

AUREON INSTITUTE   Harold Streitfeld
71 Park Avenue   Director
New York, N.Y. 10016

WAINWRIGHT HOUSE   John S. Gillooly
Milton Point   Director
Rye, N.Y. 10580

HUMAN DIMENSIONS INSTITUTE   Jeanne Rindge
at Rosary Hill College   President and
4380 Main Street   Executive Director
Buffalo, N.Y. 14226

PLAINFIELD CONSULTATION CENTER   Lawrence Kesner
831 Madison Avenue   Exec. Dir.
Plainfield, N.J. 07060   Natalie Mann,
                                           Dir. of Services

BUCKS COUNTY SEMINAR HOUSE   Grenville Moat
Erwinna, Pa. 18920   Director

INSTITUTE FOR RATIONAL LIVING   Kurt Konietzko
Pennsylvania Branch
300 South 19th Street
Philadelphia, Pa. 19103

CENTER FOR THE WHOLE PERSON   William Swartley
1633 Race Street   Director
Philadelphia, Pa. 19103

ASSOCIATES FOR HUMAN RESOURCES   John B. Marvin, Director
387 Sudbury Road   Wendy Wyatt, Director
Concord, Mass. 01742

R.F.D. 1   Winthrop Puffer
Newmarket, New Hampshire 03810

INSTITUTE FOR EXPERIMENTAL   Robert & Niela Horn
EDUCATION
P.O. Box 446
Lexington, Mass. 02173

CUMBRES   Cesareo Pelaez
Box C   President
Dublin, New Hampshire 03444

THE FAMILY RELATIONS INSTITUTE   Lori Eisenberg
3509 Farm Hill Drive   Director
Falls Church, Virginia 22044

ORIZON INSTITUTE   Barbara Mullens
2710 36th Street, N.W.   President
Washington, D.C. 20007

ADANTA   James Emerson
1298 Talcott Place   President
Decatur, Georgia 30033

THE CENTER OF MAN   Sidney Jourard, Theodore
Micanopy, Fla. 32667   Landaman, Vincent
                                                                           O'Connell

CANADA AND MEXICO

SHALAL   Lee Pulos
750 West Broadway   Director
Vancouver, B.C.

COLD MOUNTAIN INSTITUTE   Richard Weaver
P.O. Box 4362   Ernest Stickel
Edmonton 60, Alberta

STRATHMERE   R. Alex Sim
North Gower
Ontario, Canada

SYNERGIA   Marie Brewer
P.O. Box 1685, Station B.   Director
Montreal 2, Quebec

YOLOTLI   Alice Goldring
Sierra Vertientes 365
Mexico D.F. 10, Mexico